OVERCOMING
OCD & DEPRESSION

My Personal Journey and Recovery

Dedicated to my children, Justin and Jillian.

DAVID B. WHITE

Overcoming OCD and Depression:
My Personal Journey and Recovery

Dave White
335 Clubhouse Road
Hunt Valley, Maryland 21031
dbwhite20@yahoo.com

Library of Congress Number: 2007902438
International Standard Book Number: 978-1-60126-033-8

Front and Back Cover photos
taken by Gretchen White.

Printed by
Masthof Press
219 Mill Road
Morgantown, PA 19543-9516

Contents

Foreword..v

Words of Encouragement...............................viii

Introduction...xiii

Acknowledgments xxi

Chapter 1 - A Surreal But Scary Summer in the NFL............1

Chapter 2 - The Day of Reckoning.........................7

Chapter 3 - My Secret for You................................14

Chapter 4 - OCD and the Right Occupation.....................21

Chapter 5 - Optimism and Living with a Positive Attitude ...32

Chapter 6 - Regular Doctor Appointments 39

Chapter 7 - Cognitive Behavioral Psychotherapy.................46

Chapter 8 - Paxil and Other SSRIs (Selective Serotonin
Reuptake Inhibitors) 52

Chapter 9 - The Essential of a Proper Diet 60

Chapter 10 - Supplements that Can Change Your Life........68

Chapter 11 - Learning to Forgive Yourself.............................75

Chapter 12 - Read, Read, Read 83

Chapter 13 - Surround Yourself Only With People
Who Love You...88

Chapter 14 - Exercise and Staying Active...................................95

Chapter 15 - Procrastination and Staying Organized.........101

Chapter 16 - Support Groups...104

Chapter 17 - Sex and Intimacy...109

Chapter 18 - Positive and Unending Energy.....................115

Chapter 19 - Good Stress and Stress that Kills..................121

Chapter 20 - Conclusion..130

References 134

Foreword

He had me fooled. I had known Dave White for more than a year when he asked me to help him with a book. I figured that he was probably writing something about selling successfully, because that's what he does for a living and because it was the part of his life through which I met him.

So, I was tremendously surprised when I learned that he was writing a book about his own struggles with OCD. I knew about the compulsive checking of locks and doors that's associated with OCD, but I was totally unaware of the depression that's often part of the disease, and Dave is the last guy I ever would have thought of as having issues with depression.

As he says in the book, he's a Type-A personality, and I never saw him without a smile and a hearty handshake. The Dave I know is a very personable and positive guy, so he's an excellent example of someone who has worked very hard to beat OCD.

If you're suffering from this disease, use Dave's experiences as an inspiration. Have faith that you can find healing, and work hard to attain it. Then people who meet you will be amazed to learn that you ever suffered with depression.

Bill Simpson, *Editor*

OCD defined my life so many years in my life, but with the help of family, friends, medical professionals, and God, I have overcome my disease. I now lead a wonderful life, and I'm able to enjoy my life. It is so great that I can say that today because for so long, I believed I would be different than other people.

Now, let me emphasize that I will never pronounce myself "cured." OCD and depression is a disease that will always lurk within me, and if I allow myself to grow complacent, OCD could again take control of my life. While writing this book I had several weeks of a bout of OCD after feeling great for four years. I went for some blood work for a life insurance policy and feared about the results and obsessed for a couple of weeks. I was found to be healthy and instantly, I felt whole again, but the fear that had been with me reminded me of the way I felt at one time. So, instead of saying that I'm "cured," I'll say that I now have control of the disease that once had control of me. Up till the time of my blood work, I had completely forgotten what OCD felt like. I know a lot of you want to feel that way.

So let's go back to this sentence: I now lead a wonderful life, and I'm able to enjoy my life. It's the second clause in that sentence that describes the changes in my life.

While I suffered from OCD, I actually led a wonderful life, but I couldn't enjoy it completely in my mind and actions because OCD was holding me back. I could find the one cloud in the bluest sky, and I worried endlessly about things that seem foolish now. Back then, those foolish things loomed as insurmountable obstacles to my health and to my happiness.

Now, however, I'm able to see those life-limiting fears for what they really are. I'm able to enjoy and treasure my life, and I'm truly grateful for all that I have. I have a beautiful wife and healthy children and live in the rural setting of Lancaster County, Pennsylvania, and have a great job. I worked hard to get where I am today but nothing I have done has been more of an accomplishment than saying I no longer have OCD. Life is not always easy for any of us, but OCD is truly something that can hold a person back. The pages of this book hold valuable information and research that will help many with depression and OCD beat this horrible disease. Put your trust in me, because I owe it to you, my fellow human being, to help you feel at peace like I feel today. I will open up for the first time in a very long time on my trials and tribulations of my life in the hopes that you can be comforted that you can conquer OCD once and for all. I am a spiritual person and I have always believed that if you are lucky enough to heal in life, that you owe it to help others feel good instead of just being absorbed in yourself.

OCD certainly held me back. It limited my life and filled me with pointless fears. So, my hope is to help you, my fellow OCD sufferer, move past your OCD problems and gain the ability to enjoy your life. I know how overwhelming your problems can seem, and I firmly believe that the steps that have worked for me will also work for you.

It is my dream and it is very important to me that my lasting legacy will be that, during my short time on this earth, I was able to help others to feel whole again by showing them how to conquer their OCD and the other mental disorders that restricted their lives.

This book can be read for generations to come to help sufferers first self-diagnose themselves and then take care of their illness. You may not agree with all that I write, and that is ok and completely understandable. After all I do not have all the answers but I do have a lot and have helped many to feel great about their lives. But, if you take from this book some things or just one thing that changes your life, then I will have made a positive difference in your life. Is there any greater gift than giving to someone else?

Words of Encouragement

> *"At the time you were born you were given an amazing gift—a gift that most of us forget about as we grow older. It's the power to design your own unique life. You are an artist and the canvas is your life."*
>
> *—Author Cheryl Richardson*

If I died tomorrow, my obituary in the local newspaper might read something like this:

> *David Barrett White, 38, the son of Nancy and J. B. White, died yesterday of natural causes.*
>
> *He was a simple man who loved watching football and enjoyed the outdoors and his family.*
>
> *He had fulfilled his life long passion by working for the Philadelphia Eagles in Public Relations. He had previously worked as an intern with the Washington Redskins and later with the Florida Panthers in the 90's.*
>
> *He loved his country music, especially the songs of Brooks and Dunn, Travis Tritt, and the music of Aerosmith, as well as the soft music of Neil Diamond.*
>
> *As he grew up, he learned to love his family the most, and he learned many important life lessons from his mistakes. He was a resident of Lancaster, PA, and a graduate of Susquehanna University (Class of 1990). He was employed as a benefits consultant at a firm he loved—Richard J. Princinsky Associates, Inc., of Hunt Valley, Maryland.*
>
> *Dave is survived by his loving wife Gretchen, his son*

Justin, 5, and his daughter, Jillian, 3, whom he called his "Queen with Teeth."

Dave was known to have a strong Type-A personality and had a zest for life. If he was not playing sports, he was down at the bay fishing or fishing on a river, because he found his soul on the water.

His greatest accomplishment in life, though, was that he lived with Obsessive Compulsive Disorder for years and that, with the help of many, found a way to conquer it.

He authored the book Overcoming OCD and Depression: My Personal Journey and Recovery.

I can write my own obituary today and years ago there was no way I could write this on paper. I can also write this book today because my fear of dying and my compulsions from OCD have greatly dissipated. I understand why I felt the way that I did and I hope to show others why they feel the way they do. If you had asked me about dying fifteen years ago, when I was crippled by OCD, I would have told you that I was terrified and confused and really saw no light at the end of the tunnel. Many of you have picked up this book because you might be at your last wits' end of being depressed and are putting your faith in someone else's words to get better. I can help you because I was where you are today only a couple years ago.

Years ago, life became so difficult that I didn't even want to wake up in the morning. OCD would come and go often in my life. There is good depression though and then there is unhealthy depression. When your depression starts to get to the point that your work is being effected or you are struggling in school and cannot maintain your focus in life, then you have to get help. OCD symptoms would make me feel tired and would lower my self-esteem at times in my life. I was always strong-willed and always demanded that I be successful in my life and would settle for nothing less.

Now, I have gotten to the end of the tunnel and I see the light. Life is good, and I can tell you that I feel very happy and intact inside. And, although OCD has been a constant battle, I have accomplished so much in life and will continue to do so. The scary thoughts and obsessions that were such a part of my daily life are gone and I feel as though I can do anything I want to accomplish these days. I want you to be able to rid your life of OCD, and by reading this book you are taking the first step toward beating OCD.

I remember my Dad telling me a great saying that my grandfather would say to him. It's become the saying that I live by, "Once you die, they are going to bury you six feet deep for a long time, so make it happen in life today."

After all, we are all born unto this earth and we will all die someday, but the legacy that we leave is so important. Life for everyone can be a roller coaster ride with its ups and downs, but I will help you realize that you can beat depression by the things you do. I can help you get healthy physically and mentally because there are things I have done the last five years of my life and I live a great life. And, of course, we all hope that we will live a good and happy life. Then when we leave this earth we can live with God someday (if you believe in God), to continue to be happy. All I ask is that as you read this book start to make changes to your life today, not tomorrow. You will not get better if you do not tackle OCD today.

My biggest commitment to you, the reader, is to bring to you the results of my research and my personal experiences, to help you to understand OCD, and to walk away from it as I have. We can do this together, through this book, so that your life will change only for the better. You will have to have a strong desire to get better and will have to work hard but the hard work will pay off.

I do not have all the answers for the sufferers of this debilitating disorder, but I do know that I have some crucial answers because I have suffered from the disease and taken control of it. When I had OCD, I so much wanted to find a book that could give me hope and promise, and this book is the kind I always looked for. For many years I dreamed about writing this book and another author pushed me to write the book and it became a reality.

I desperately wanted someone to tell me that I wasn't the only one with the disease. I desperately wanted to know that someone had overcome OCD. I desperately wanted assurance, that I could overcome my problems and fears. I never found that book, so I feel blessed to be able to write it for the millions of others with this disease.

I truly want to help you. I know that you may be confused and scared at this time in your life, as I was so many years ago. I want to help you understand OCD and depression and how to beat it. So much of depression is because of the chemical makeup of your brain and if you can learn how to put more of these chemicals in your brain, you can heal quickly. You will beat OCD if you have the desire to work hard and if you will listen to many of the mental health professionals and doctors who are out there. Some people will be able to get better through therapy but if you are prescribed an anti-depressant or another kind of medication keep on taking it because the meditation can change your life.

Your life will change if you are willing to treat yourself with extreme self-care and to love yourself enough to say, "I do not want to feel the pains of OCD anymore. I'm done with being depressed. Today is the day I am going to be committed to myself and to my loved ones to get better. Not next week or a month from now but I am going to work on my depression today."

So read the pages of this book because no one deserves

to live with OCD or any form of depression. I will always be here for anyone who wants my help.

Here is a quote that I read recently, and as you read the pages of this book keep it in mind. It reads like this and it was said by a man named Robert Half:

"Persistence is what makes the impossible possible, the possible likely, and the likely definite."

Persist and you will succeed.

INTRODUCTION

Have any of these things ever happened in your life? Have these thoughts ever stopped you in your tracks and scared you so badly, that you shook from your head to your toes and wondered why you were having such thoughts?

Have you ever . . .

1. Felt for no reason that you might be dying from cancer, Aids, a brain tumor, or some other horrible or terminal disease?

2. Felt that you cannot move forward in life because you're scared of the next move that you might make in life?

3. Moved objects around on a table or desk several times, until you felt comfortable with where you had placed them?

4. Felt that you had to clean everything around you always, like your home or your car, and be organized all the time to be able to function?

5. Gone downstairs several times during the night to check the stove, or the locks on your doors, or your fireplace, to make sure the house would not burn down while you were sleeping?

6. Obsessed about religion and God and feared the subject of the Devil and then feared the numbers 666?

7. Counted numbers incessantly in your head (1, 2, 3, 4, 5, etc.) in an endless number routine?

8. Seen a knife, felt a fear, and been scared that you had thought that you might harm someone for no reason? Although this action rarely happens with violence, the thought and why you had it, really scared you.

9. Washed your hands many times because of the fear of having germs and contaminants on your hands?

10. Been on a plane as you hit turbulence and felt sure that the nose of the plane was going to turn downward and crash to the earth?

11. Gotten a fork in a restaurant and, even though it looked clean, been so afraid that it was infected with germs that you had to clean it before you used it?

12. Hit a pothole in the road and sworn that you hit someone, then driven back just to feel comfortable that you did not?

If you've had these experiences or feelings a lot, then chances are strong that you're feeling the insecurities that I felt when I was afflicted with Obsessive Compulsive Disorder. I felt normal as a person a lot of the time but then at other times I would become obsessed with these kinds of thoughts. You know that you shouldn't be feeling this way, and you wish you could control yourself from thinking these thoughts. You just can't get these bizarre thoughts out of your mind.

If you've had these thoughts a lot, then OCD is definitely limiting your life and all that you can be. But there is hope, because as you will learn there are chemicals or lack of chemicals in the brain that made you feel this way, and today OCD is understood much better than ever before.

Research described on a website from a company called Brain Matters Imaging Centers, has shown that OCD can occur because of a breakdown in the communication path between the front part of the brain, or frontal lobe, and deeper structures (the basal ganglia). There are things that you will be able to do to allow these parts of your brain to communicate better. As you learn to do this you will learn to feel more control of your thoughts and actions, and for some, OCD and depression will dissipate.

Some of the studies that Brain Matter Imaging Centers mentioned, showed that it takes an average of 17 years from the time OCD begins for some people to obtain proper treatment. This happened to me and I do not want you to suffer with OCD as long as I did, before getting the proper help. I suffered with OCD during the 1980's at different times in high school and college and was misdiagnosed by some doctors because OCD was not well-known. You will learn to live in the magic of life and most importantly let's do it quickly for you.

I know these feelings of OCD, and I know that eight million other Americans are currently suffering from this debilitating condition. I recently read a report that said perhaps one in fifty adults in the U.S. may have OCD or have had it at some time. And, it's highly likely that millions more suffer from this disease but hide it from others because of the fear that people will think they are crazy. Running around and telling people about some thoughts that you are having is just not something many are going to do. Many are not willing to let others know that they are having bizarre thoughts because everyone feels they have to be perfect. But you know what, no one is, and no one will ever be perfect.

You should realize that OCD is a chemical imbalance

within chemicals in the brain like dopamine and serotonin and the neurotransmitters in the brain, and if you receive proper treatment, you will not think these crazy thoughts nearly as frequently. It is encouraging that today they know about these chemicals and if they know that, then they are so close to curing depression.

Another part of the struggles of OCD sufferers, is that, in my opinion, many doctors do not have the proper training to diagnose it. Many doctors that I went to in the 80's and 90's missed my OCD because nervous conditions and depression, as mentioned before, were not as well-known as they are today. Many articles and books written during the last ten years have allowed more practitioners to ask the right questions and to learn more about OCD and how to treat it. I have even talked with many doctors, who are now more educated about OCD and depression. Sure they deal with depression a lot these days because society is really stressed but some doctors may have not dealt as much with OCD. It was refreshing to talk with some of my doctors and really explain to them from my heart what OCD and depression felt like so that maybe they would understand other patients who would come in with the disorder.

So, it's highly likely that millions of other Americans and people worldwide have OCD, but have kept the affliction their own personal secret. Let's face it, we all have our pride, and admitting a fault is one of the hardest things for many people to do—particularly men and I can say that because I am one. We have to learn to open up if we are depressed and reach out either to loved ones or to doctors and keep pride out of it and say "I need help."

At first, I had a huge problem admitting to friends and family members that I had OCD because that admission would have made me look vulnerable and weak. Inside I was a determined person and I learned to live with OCD, but hated the feeling more than you can imagine. I fought the internal battle by myself for a long time. So I fought the thoughts endlessly, until I finally went to my family doctor and my psychologist and said that I was tired and needed some help.

OCD thoughts can scare a person to death because the person knows that these thoughts are a big waste of time. It drives you nuts to think that you are wasting away your life thinking about needless things, but you have to do it to feel normal. But, if the person does not perform the OCD rituals—if he doesn't check the locks on the door 5 times or wash his hands 7 times—and if the person does not give proper attention to the useless thoughts, life seems to stand still and will not move ahead until he goes through his rituals.

When I finally opened up and acknowledged I had an uncontrollable problem, I felt like a person who one day admits that he is gay and comes out of the closet. The person then says, "This is who I am, and this is how I feel and damn it, people are going to accept me for who I am."

Finally, in my teen years, I opened up and talked about how I felt. I described the fears that had limited my life. I moved past the shame and accepted the fact that I had the disease called Obsessive Compulsive Disorder. In my case, I had a severe case of the disease, and my first step in moving past it was to admit that, I myself, had it and to allow myself to accept help from others. That wasn't easy, but it was worthwhile.

Now, after doing years of research on depression and OCD, I have learned that OCD can be hereditary. Like cholesterol, it can be passed down through the generations of families. I remember when I heard that, I realized that I was not different, but I was like others in my family. Others, who I later found out throughout my family tree, had had OCD.

OCD can also begin because of a tragic event in one's life. The loss of a loved one, breaking up with a boyfriend or a girlfriend, a divorce, and a car accident are examples of things that can sometimes trigger OCD. If you suspect that such an event has brought on your bout of OCD, or if you believe that it's hereditary, have confidence that you can heal and feel emotionally normal again.

I've read many books written by wonderful psychologists and doctors and by other people who have dealt with OCD in their practices. But the books that have touched me the most are the ones from the sufferers themselves, because they actually lived with OCD and had many of the fears that I once did.

Many of the books that I read were from psychologists, who talked about their personal experiences of dealing with patients. I knew how these patients themselves felt, because they had many of the fears that I had most of my life.

However, I always wanted to read a book that would not only tell me about the effects of OCD, but would show me how I could be cured. Reading the pages of books that talked about the many symptoms of OCD were not going to get me better because I knew the symptoms. I wanted to be cured and I wanted to read words that would cure me now. Because I never found such a book about how to heal, I have chosen to write about my experiences and how I have overcome my OCD. I do not have a Ph.D. but I have had OCD. I have lived with it and I know a lot about it. So, my motivation for writing this book is my belief that my experiences will help you overcome your OCD.

To me, the difference between a book on OCD by a psychologist and a book about OCD by a sufferer is similar to the difference between a book about hurricanes by a scientist and a book by someone who has lived through a hurricane. Classroom theory and real-life experience are drastically different. Both have value, but a person who has been there can certainly provide valuable insights than someone who hasn't been there can possibly offer.

I suffered from OCD, so I have firsthand knowledge of

the disease. In addition and I mention about hurricanes, because I was actually in Florida on the day when Hurricane Andrew brought horrific destruction. The experience of being in a house and wondering if you'll survive those 140 MPH winds is infinitely more terrifying than watching a hurricane on television. And, just as the person who watches a hurricane on TV doesn't really know what it's like to wonder if you'll live to see another day, the person who studies OCD, may not really know what it's like to live with the disease.

I believe that reading my words will help you to realize that you are not alone with your feelings of OCD. I have been where you are in your life, and trust me, from the bottom of my soul, when I say that you will feel wonderful some day, even though right now you can't believe that, you will feel right. Of course, if you currently feel that OCD is your "normal," then look forward to a much better life ahead. Learn to get up and start your day saying that "I am done with OCD and I will kick its ass."

Sometimes I feel that I missed out on some important things in the first thirty years of my life. I don't dwell on those thoughts, but I do use them as motivation to make up on some lost time in my next thirty years. You can do the same. I do not take life for granted. I travel and have great friends and enjoy each and every day of this life and will do it to make up for some lost time.

In this book I am going to describe every thought that I had and every painful experience that I had during my OCD years. I am not ashamed of them and some of you may have many of the same ones I had. I will talk about some of them so that you can be comforted that you are no different than me or anyone else. Although my experiences may be different from yours in some ways, I know that they're similar in their power to fill us with fear and to take so much of the joy out of our lives.

So, good luck and keep the faith because you will make it and beat OCD or depression. I did. You will too.

David White
Lititz, PA
dbwhite20@yahoo.com

ACKNOWLEDGMENTS

I try to read a quote a day to build wisdom, wherever I am, and a lot of those quotes are in my day timer. This daily organizer is truly a book I could not live without, and I would be lost without it. It has thoughts at the top of the Franklin Covey daily pages for its users to stop and think about, before their day begins. Many of the quotes which I have read there have really had strong impacts on my life and have made me think about life in general. One, which I read recently, really had me stop and think and appreciate two special people in my life—my wife, Gretchen, and my own Mother. This is the quote:

"We bear the world and we make it . . . There was never a great man who had not a great mother—it is hardly an exaggeration." –Olive Schreiner

I read this and could not help but think of my own Mom and the mother of my own children, Gretchen. Both of these women have enough love in them for ten women and have shown me what true love is. From the time I came into this world, I have never been loved by someone more than my own mother, Nancy White. She has been my security blanket and my personal bodyguard, all wrapped into one. If she could help it, she refused to allow anyone to hurt me from the time I came into this great and fabulous world.

When I was a young boy, she lifted me up and constantly let me know that I could accomplish anything that I put my mind to, and she made me feel that I was a remarkable young man. Because of her unending dedication and support, I have been able to accomplish so much in my life.

As I grew up, she felt a need to leave my own father for several reasons, but mainly because she could not live with a man who did not have the same love in his heart for me, as she did.

There was no one who could ever harm me while I was in elementary, high school, or college, and she instilled in me the belief that I was someone who could succeed in life, even though others did not believe in me. As a man, everyone needs that in their life to be successful in life and to be a good father themselves some day. It was she who supported me in sports, in education, and in life, and it was she who persuaded me to see the psychologist who would diagnose my OCD and get me the medication that I needed to feel normal again. No parent is perfect, but my mother is pretty darn close.

Later on in my life, Gretchen and I married and became the parents of two wonderful children. Justin is 5 and Jillian is 3, and I treat our children with the love that my own Mom gave to me as a youngster. My wife is beautiful on the outside and, most important, she is more beautiful on the inside and has been there for me along the way when things were going well and when I was low and needed her support. Thank you, Gretchen, for being you.

Thanks also to my brother Chris, my womb mate, or should I say twin brother, and to my sister Heather, who have always loved me for who I am.

We may have been separated as kids but with the love of the Lord and our parents we were later reunited as one. I thank God for that because without family, it is tough to conquer this thing we call life.

My brother and sister also helped to make me who I am today. Because of his background in psychology, my brother Chris, was also the first person who helped diagnose me as potentially having OCD. We were not raised together because he lived with my father and I with my mother but that never took the love from our hearts. My sister, Heather, has always been just a phone call away to ask for advice on things, and I thank her from the bottom of my heart.

Also, thank you so much to author Jon Gordon, who, after I read his book *Energy Addict*, has become a good friend. He helped me to realize that positive energy is the way to live life and to succeed in life. I have continued to heal with OCD and have learned so much about the ways to live life from his writing. He is the inspiration that enables me to think and complete this book. I read his book on the way home from a business trip in North Carolina and never thought reading a book would change my life as it did. I want this book to be a book that will change lives, as well. Jon's life and his writings on maintaining energy spiritually, mentally, and physically have helped me to look at life in a different perspective.

I also want to thank the Universal Athletic Club in Lancaster, Pennsylvania, and its owner Rick, for allowing me to have a gym I can workout in to free my mind and spirit.

I would be remiss not to mention such great friends and loved ones that have crossed my path in life. These people have made my life so great and filled it will such great memories. Lenny Varn (my brother-in-law), Frank Tanki, Turner Producer Howard Zalkowitz, Pete Serell, Al Giacoio (did not come to my wedding but made my book), Keith Mekenney, Brian Floyd, Chad Houck, Tommy Bold, Gary Lamb, Lynne Watson (my boss), and Dr. Bruce Miller, Ph.D., who always accepted me for who I was and was like a father to me. Also my Susquehanna University roommates Brock Mowery and Jeff Jakubik, who made my life at college so much fun. Also a special thanks to Bob Lange, Derrick Boyko, Rich Burg, and the rest of the Public and Media Relations Department with the Philadelphia Eagles, who have allowed me to experience working in the NFL. Thank you to Dr. John Palumbo and Dr. Julie Burrowes, in Lancaster, who listened to me when I was scared with OCD and helped to get me on the medication I needed to live a great life. Even though my OCD troubled me at different times in my life, I had friends, such as Barry Axe, and local doctors, to talk with and accept me for who I was. I love all of you for that.

And last but not least I would like to thank the Good Lord upstairs, because without Him in my life, I am nothing. If you met me you would not believe I was a spiritual person but as I have aged I have realized that God gave me OCD for a reason. He is the power who gave me the family and friends I have in this lifetime. I could have been born into another family and had different people in my life but I am so glad I wasn't. All these great people made me the man that I am today.

Chapter 1

A Surreal But Scary Summer in the NFL

"Is Life worth living? Aye, with the best of us, heights of us, depths of us—Life is the test of us!"
—Lorraine Roosevelt Robinson

Since I was a young kid, I had dreamed of working in the NFL. This dream has remained with me since I was six years old. My idol as a child was Roger Staubach, quarterback for the Dallas Cowboys, and I wanted to someday work with athletes of his caliber. It did not matter what I did for an NFL team but I have always had such a passion to work in the NFL.

My dream became a reality in 1988, while I was a junior in college. I went into training camp with the Washington Redskins as a 20-year-old kid, and had a summer I will remember for the rest of my life. I remember the exhilaration I had in my heart and body the day I got a letter from the Washington Redskins saying that they were interested in me working for them for eight weeks during the summer. When I ended up getting to training camp at Dickinson College, in Carlisle, Pennsylvania, I was hanging around players with the likes of Art Monk, Gary Clark, and Mark Rypien, the great offensive line called "The Hogs" and they were players I grew up watching through my youth. I think I smiled most of the time I was up at camp because I had a feeling of excitement that I was working in the NFL with the Redskins.

That same summer, however, I fought through several episodes of OCD, that held me back from having that perfect summer. I bring up this story because you will probably recognize some of the OCD issues I had suffered with that summer. We all have stories like this that were difficult but I look back on them now because I was able to move on and laugh about it. I was living a glorious moment in my young life that millions of kids my age only dreamed of, working in the NFL, but an incident weeks before training camp began changed my life forever. A week before I left to go to Redskins camp, I was down at the shore in Avalon, NJ, partying with some friends, like I did every summer. Avalon was and has always been a place of peace for me in my heart and in my soul and as a kid I spent many summers at this great beach resort town.

Unfortunately, I was wrestling with Derek, a buddy of mine in our shore house. It got rough, and he accidently cracked my head into the side of a wall, and I sustained a mild concussion. I was dazed and confused most of the rest of the trip. I remember getting home and lying in bed, and I continued to be confused. Fear overcame me like never before because with the concussion I could not control my thoughts. I let my fears of the mind get carried away and basically made a mound out of an ant hill. The room I was in was spinning and I was scared. I was also planning to leave for the Redskins' training camp in only a couple of days.

The biggest issues I had with OCD was that I obsessed incessantly about my health and was constantly afraid that I was dying. For days, like someone has with a concussion, I was very confused and nervous because I was not thinking clearly. I had a diagnosis from my family doctor of a mild concussion but in my mind I swore I had a brain hemorrhage and worried a lot about it before leaving and while in camp. Here I was having the time of my life but being held back by the fears that I had an incurable condition.

Most people would have accepted it as nothing more than a slight concussion and moved on, but not I. This injury scared me to death, even though I had been an athlete and had concussions in the past. The excitement of being with the Redskins was coming and I think when the accident happened I let my OCD step into trying to control the nervousness I had of going to training camp. Anyone at my age then would have had apprehensive fears like I had but I made them a lot worse.

This time, however, a mild concussion had me fearing that I might be dying. I let this incident bother me for the week before I left for camp and it lasted through some of training camp. People with OCD can obsess a great deal about their health or other things because they are programmed to act in that manner. I was feeling so frustrated because I kept trying to tell myself that all I had was a concussion and not to make such a big deal about it. But my brain would just keep obsessing about it on and on.

There I was, fulfilling a dream of traveling with a football team on flights and living in a dorm with star players for weeks, and I let a bruise to my head scare me beyond belief. Sure, I had a great time, but I spent a lot of unwanted time worrying about a mild concussion. I could just not accept that eventually it was going to go away and I would feel normal again. It took some time for me to forgive myself for allowing myself to even for a second, ruin what was such an unbelievable chapter in my life. These kinds of things happened to me a lot when I was young, but why did it have to happen when I was at training camp with a professional football team?

I needed to be reassured that I was all right, so I had the Redskins' team doctors check me two or three times to be certain that I did not have a brain hemorrhage or bleeding on the brain. The doctors repeatedly told me that I had probably shifted my brain a little bit, and that was why my equilibrium and balance was off and why I felt a little confused. They probably got sick of worrying about me when they had players to attend to but I needed that reassurance.

I had the assurance of some excellent doctors that I was fine, but I had to keep checking and seeking reassurance, that I would be all right. I think I was so excited to be in camp and it was so surreal to be with the Redskins that the concussion made my OCD go somewhat out of whack. The timing of getting hurt stunk and if it happened to me today I could deal with it head on. But I was suffering from OCD and my obsessions were going a little crazy because I was young.

I was frustrated with myself because I was allowing myself to feel so worried even though I had gotten confirmation that I was all right. Despite the assurances from the doctors, I obsessed about my concussion almost constantly while I was at camp.

I clearly remember being angry with myself because I was working long days with the Redskins and giving it all I had, but then I would worry that something was seriously wrong with me. When I was not working or was alone in my dorm room, I could allow myself to feel such fear. I was so high and then at times low.

This experience is certainly familiar to many of the readers of this book. Someone with OCD can drive himself nuts worrying about his/her health. I was a hypochondriac at that time, and OCD can make hypochondria ten times worse. I would worry about my health and then question why I allowed my life to be caught up in worrying about my health. It was truly a negative circle I was in.

Luckily for me, I ended up meeting a friend and later a girlfriend that summer. She was a good athlete and a soccer player and was beautiful, and we had a lot of fun that summer while at camp.

When I was with her that summer, it seemed like I could forget about some of the fears I had and the things that I was worrying about—thank God! I was a college kid and she was younger and was just a really nice person and we just had a lot of fun. She would come over and watch movies and ESPN sports at night in my dorm and those days were a lot of fun. Here I was working in the NFL and had a great girl to hang with at night and a refrigerator full of beer. What else could a 20-year-old guy ask for his life?

When you have OCD, you obsess about your health because you want to try to get control of your feelings and of your life. This is really true when you are anxious about something or there is a lot of stress in your life. I think I was so excited about being with the Skins and just wished OCD had not shown itself while I was there.

Many of you who are reading these pages probably suffer today, from what I suffered from years ago. Trust me when I tell you, that you too, will feel whole again and that you will not worry about your health incessantly forever. Trust me when I tell you that I obsessed about my health that summer and for many years afterward, but I do not obsess today. I certainly take care of my health, but it's no longer an obsession. Over the last ten years of my life I have made changes to my diet, been on some medication, and made exercise a prerequisite for my life to help me with my depression. I accepted a long time ago that I wanted to take the right vitamins and exercise and do what I needed to do but someday I will die and I am at peace with that.

Now, I let life take its course. I understand that I am healthy and since going on the right medication, I do not worry about my health, as I once did. If you feel like I did that summer, do yourself the most important favor you can do and reach out to a doctor or a psychologist and do not wait. Medical professionals can help you with either referring you to a psychologist or a specialist deals with mental disorders. Act now, because your silent suffering will strip you of so many special moments and waste some precious years of your life, and you cannot get those years back.

If you experience constant stress or are struggling with depression, a regular checkup with a doctor is something that you owe to yourself and to your body. If you are ever diagnosed with depression, make it a point to check in with your doctors on a regular basis so that they can make decisions on the direction you want to go with your health. Without your health, as I will mention in this book countless times, you really have nothing.

It is good to have your blood pressure checked and to have your weight checked for fluctuations and to allow the doctors to know if you are sleeping and eating right. Changes in your health could be a sign for the doctors that they need to change your medications, if you are put on them for depression and anxiety.

I know because I worked closely with my doctors for the last couple of years, and now I feel so good every day. For a long time I tried to talk my doctors out of not putting me on medication but for me I finally gave in because I had to control the chemical imbalances I had in my brain. In fact, people who meet me now find it quite surprising to learn that I have struggled with OCD and had depression. I live such a positive life and have come so far since the days of my fear of dying during that summer with the Redskins.

Chapter 2

The Day of Reckoning

"We can't do much about the length of our lives, but we do plenty about its width and depth."

—Evan Esar

For as long as I can remember, it seemed that I lived with a partner on my shoulder, called OCD (Out of Control Demon). This demon, AKA Obsessive Compulsive Disorder, would never leave me alone in my thoughts and actions. Wherever I went, and wherever my thoughts went, OCD always came along, an uninvited and completely unwelcome guest, whose only purpose was to take the joy out of my life.

Obsessive Compulsive Disorder is a problem that I share with nearly eight million other Americans. That number shows that OCD is a very common mental disorder today, and because OCD is now so common, sufferers no longer have to feel that everyone else is normal and they are alone in dealing with their demons. Know that today you can flick that demon off your shoulder and get help.

People with this disorder experience different kinds of obsessions, which come in the form of unwanted thoughts that can control their lives. To combat the unwanted thoughts, they have to complete compulsive rituals such as checking locks or repeatedly washing their hands, just to relieve them of their unwanted thoughts.

My condition was mild enough that, as a young man, I was able to hide my feelings from friends and family and even from my psychologist for a long time. Deep inside, however, I knew that something was wrong. I continued to think some scary and bizarre thoughts, and I did rituals to chase those thoughts. While that was going on though, I was very successful in sports and was able to maintain good grades all through school.

When I was growing up in the 1970's and 1980's, little was known about OCD. Because it was such an unknown disorder, explaining my OCD made me feel weird and isolated from everyone else. I knew I was not feeling right with my thoughts and found it very difficult to tell people exactly how I felt. So I did what many people do and that is to fight the internal battle inside themselves.

I would sit in a psychologist's office and explain that I sometimes felt out-of-control and that I was frequently washing my hands and checking things in my house to alleviate my weird thoughts. I would talk with him about the nights when I would lie in bed and then make my way down the stairs to check the stove, fireplace, and locks to make sure the house was secure. Unfortunately, one-time checks were rarely enough. More frequently, I would perform my rituals two or three times during the night.

My best friend, Keith, whom I have known my whole life, would stay over and I would also ask him to check doors, locks, stoves, and refrigerators. At the time, I was the male of the household, with just my sister and my mother, but I think I checked the doors and locks more than what was normal. To this day he and I can now laugh, but those expeditions I would take through my house before bed were crazy. I was doing these obsessions at night to relieve some of my compulsions that were going on in my head. It was amazing that Keith didn't think that I should be in the funny farm.

I remember Keith speaking at my rehearsal dinner the night before my wedding. My Mom asked all my tightest friends to speak about something that they always remembered about me. I remember Keith standing up and saying that I always took on the father role in our family and would check doors and locks and windows to protect my family. I remember sitting next to my beautiful wife Gretchen at the dinner and thinking, "Man, I snowed him."

I may have checked the doors for burglars but the other stuff was done to feel sane again and to chase my obsessive thoughts. Anyone with OCD, because we are alike, will totally understand why I did what I did those nights before I would go to bed. If I did not perform some of those rituals there is no way that I could of fallen asleep. My mind just simply could not have been able to rest and be at peace.

My psychologist at the time was a man named Bruce Miller. Through the years I have always had him to talk to when my OCD symptoms have gotten tough or when I have had fears in my life. Bruce knew that I sometimes struggled with control issues because I had come from a sometimes dysfunctional family and because I was not able to grow up with my twin brother after my parents had divorced. He basically knew me inside and out and I learned how to heal because of him.

It wasn't until I was in my thirties, that this same psychologist and my own brother Chris, would collectively diagnose me as having symptoms of OCD. I had gotten married and two years later had a son, Justin. I visited Bruce because I was feeling scared with having a new baby in my life. I was scared to death to be a Daddy because I knew that my life was going to be changing drastically and this anxiety brought on some uncomfortable bouts with OCD.

I was anxious because I was entering a new stage of my life, and my anxiety brought on some OCD feelings. It was at that moment, that I said to Bruce that my brother and I had been talking a lot and that I thought I definitely had symptoms of OCD. Like throwing yourself before the mercy of a judge, I threw myself before Bruce and let him know I was struggling and needed help.

This was the first time ever he had talked to me about going on medication called selective serotonin reuptake inhibitors, or SSRIs. At first I said there was no way I was going to take a medication like Paxil or Zoloft, and that I could beat this mental disorder on my own. Why not? I had done it for nearly fifteen years and I could beat it myself. Or so I thought.

For me, as with most men, admitting that I had a problem was not an easy thing to do. Bruce told me that he strongly suggested that I should have some blood work done and talk with my doctor about the ramifications and benefits of taking an antidepressant. Bruce felt that I had been through so many episodes with OCD coming and going in my life that I needed to see if an antidepressant could curb my depression.

I clearly remember walking out of his office, through the door that I had walked through so many times before, and thinking that maybe we were finally on to something. I thought maybe if I went on the medication that just maybe I would feel better and that I was not going to fight it any longer.

The next day I got up the courage to call my doctor and make an appointment. I decided I was not going to let any other days go by because I may talk myself out of going to the doctor to go on medication.

I remember the secretary saying, "And what do we need to see you for?" I conjured up my strength and my manly attitude and said, "I need to see the doctor for something really personal and I would really be comfortable just coming in and talking with him." She calmly said she understood and said, "Ok, Mr. White. That would be fine. And can you come in at 9 a.m. tomorrow morning?"

I remember going in to my doctor before work the next day, dressed in a suit on my way to work. I had a knot in the pit of my stomach, and I was shaking like a leaf because I was excited but nervous that I was going to open up a subject I had denied for so long. A nurse checked my weight and took my blood pressure, stating that it was a little higher than normal. Little did she know I was holding fifteen years of pent-up frustration and aggravation that was not going to be hidden anymore. She calmly stated again, "And what are we here to see the doctor for?" I had hidden my feelings for fifteen years, so why not for another five minutes?

"Ma'am," I said. "I am here to talk with the doctor about something really personal and I was not comfortable communicating it through the office."

She responded that she totally understood and would get the doctor. The nurse took me back to the room and probably thought I was there with a sexually transmitted disease or something that I was only comfortable to talk with a man about. My wonderful doctor, Dr. Palumbo, calmly came in and took a seat and said, "What is going on, Dave? We haven't seen you in a while and it sounds like you have something you want to discuss with me."

I remember driving to the doctor's office, practicing what I would say, and resolving that I would sternly say, "I have a problem and I think it's something mental" and that I wanted to be man enough to tell him what it was.

Instead, like my daughter Jillian wanting a snack, my body went limp, my eyes welled up, and tears came down my face like I had not cried in a long time. My face was red as a tomato and I felt like I was cooking on a skillet. Fifteen years of frustration, which I had as a youth and through college, all was coming to a head, and I opened up to my doctor that I did not want it anymore. I told him that I truly believed that I was struggling with OCD and that I was so tired of fighting it. I told him that I was worn out and just could not fight the disorder anymore.

I did not hold anything back and I explained to him my symptoms of the fear of dying, my compulsive checking of things, and my many obsessive thoughts. I told him that I was there to say, "No more!"

I remember him looking at this 6'2" 235-pound guy with a look of compassion in his eyes and saying, "Let's see what we can do for you." I handed him my psychologist Bruce's business card and said, "He thinks it's about time you and he talk and do this for me."

Without hesitation, my doctor asked a nurse to draw some blood to check on enzyme levels in my liver. He promised that he would call my psychologist and talk with him. He left the room and came back with samples of Paxil, because he felt that he would try this medicine first with me. He only put me on 30 mg. of Paxil as they were just going to start to introduce my body to a new antidepressant. He said that we would try some different SSRIs if need be, to see which of them would work the best for me.

He explained that I would take the Paxil (30 mg.) for two weeks and then come back for more blood work. He told me that they would periodically check my liver function to make sure my liver was correctly absorbing the medication.

He told me that we would start on some low doses and see if after two weeks I noticed if the OCD that hampered me for so long had showed any sign of subsiding. I remember thinking, "Did he say that we would see if the OCD would subside some?" I could not believe that it might actually go away and that I may actually not have the symptoms in my life anymore. Could that really be true?

After the doctor's appointment, I went into the bathroom and fixed my tie in the mirror and thought I was doing something special for myself and that a weight seemed to have come off my chest. I walked out of that office with a smile you might see on a quarterback after winning a Super Bowl. I had decided that I wanted to conquer OCD head on and that the time to start, was now, and the road to recovery was just starting.

After the two weeks, to my disappointment, I was not perfect, but I noticed that my symptoms had definitely gotten better. Everyone is different and the prescriptions can react differently with others, but I felt like a new man because I was at least feeling that I was getting better.

Chapter 3

My Secret for You

"Whatever the mind can conceive it can achieve."
                                    —W. Clemmons Stone

"Imagination is everything. It is the preview of life's coming attractions."
                                    —Albert Einstein

For the first time in a very long time, I opened up to you about some of the stories of my experience at training camp with the Washington Redskins and about how I was diagnosed with having OCD. I opened up to you that with the birth of my son, OCD and depression came into my life because I was so nervous about becoming a new Dad.

I needed to do that because those experiences in my life are what eventually led me to writing this book. Many people in my life will be surprised when they read about the experiences I had, because I never shared those stories with them. But now it is time for me to completely open up and talk about what I did to recover from OCD and depression because together I want you to heal and walk away from OCD like I have. I promise that as you read the rest of the book you can put some of the things I will mention to practice and hopefully for many, things will change in your life immediately. That is why I set out on my quest to write this book.

One of the most awe-inspiring and mystical gifts I can bring to you as you recover from OCD and depression is my own secret that I would be remiss if I did not mention it to you.

All I ever wanted, like I mentioned before, when I read books and magazines about OCD and depression, was to read books that would allow me to heal because life was tough. I wanted to find secrets right away so I did not have to feel the fear and insecurities that I woke up with every day. I list this secret in the beginning of this book, because I believe lives can be healed right away if you trust me. You have decided to read the pages of this book because you or a loved one may need help. I will share with you my secret and different secrets I did towards my own healing, because of my love of people and please listen to my words. This first step to recovery could change your life immediately and what I am going to tell you will change the way you think and function daily. Some of you might be saying "What is it?"

The secret is to go out and purchase the book or CD book *The Secret*, written by the great author, Rhonda Byrne. This woman's words can help you become what you always have wanted and maybe chase away your depression. Many people love self-help books and read them and make recommendations of books to friends, co-workers, and family. Sometimes you will read a book and it will affect you but maybe not others. This book is so powerful and its words changed my life overnight! It has helped me control my thoughts like never before. I do have to admit though that I understand what Byrne has written in her book and already I have felt better mentally after reading her book, but there are still probably going to be some who question her theories about the "LAW OF AT-TRACTION."

The book *The Secret*, by Byrne, has been one of the most positive books for my life and maybe yours if you want to make changes to your life right now. Not tomorrow—but now. If anything, she talks about how people can bring good to themselves through positive thinking. She talks about positive things like buying a new house or getting more healthy or having better relationships can happen by thinking positive thoughts. "Like will attract like." It has been refreshing to read this book that is intended to help people instead of watching the news about murder and killings or watching or reading horror stories. People across the world are reading her book or buying the CD book, because they are wanting so much to change their lives. I believe we all think about how we can live better lives every day we breathe.

Everyday, in our own lives, we run into non-believers and or people who refuse to believe in anything they cannot see. If something does not hit them upside the head, they do not believe something is reality. For instance, some people stand hard that they do not believe in a Jesus Christ or God, because they have not seen him in person. The Law of Attraction, is not a law you can hold in your hand. You have to count on past accounts in books and manuscripts, of the stories of famous Instead of having a negative frame of mind, I choose to follow some of the beliefs of this Law. I would be a fool, not only to flood my mind, with positive enduring thoughts, to see if they would come into fruition. Why not give this law of attraction a fling and see if it works. I tried it, and amazing things started to occur and my life changed in such a short period of time.

I followed one of the suggestions of the Law of Attraction and that was imaging. Imaging has been used by many atheletes for years where you think in your mind an event that is going to happen later in your life and it happens just like you had thought about.   I thought about, and solely focused on working hard to double my individual income I currently have. My benefits business, working for the Eagles, and the publishing of this book has been great, and financially I am very, very far from Donald Trump, but I live comfortably. To accomplish my goal of making more money, to give to my family and enjoy more from life, I focused my mind on more financial success. I took a dollar bill and wrote down the dollar amount, I would love to make in the next year. The Law of Attraction, talked about in, The Secret, mentions putting a dollar amount on a dollar bill and thinking religiously, on that amount of money. Before I knew it, I had literally stumbled into a favorable business opportunity that appears to have a bright light at the end of the tunnel.

One day recently, my daughter Jillian and I were in the small town of Manheim, PA, outside of Lancaster, PA, and my daughter begged me to stop in a McDonald's for lunch. She, like all kids, likes the burgers and fries but was 100% more interested in the kid's meal gift, that accompanied it. I almost did not go in, but she kept piping up from the back seat that she really wanted her "Mickey D's". I went in because I was not in the mood to win a battle with a three year old that I wanted her to not eat fast food on that day. She won the battle and quite honestly I owe her for pressing me to go out for lunch.

I walked up to the counter and a jovial and seemingly kind gentleman approached at the same time as I and Jillian. Some people in five seconds of meeting them, you can tell as a southern might say, "they are good people." This gentleman was a kind and considerate person, who said that I and Jillian, could be served before he and an associate. My daughter and I sat down to eat and this gentleman, I noticed, had a beautiful college ring on with a blue gem stone. I asked him if he had played college football at sometime in his life. He told me he was Frank Peterson, from West Palm Beach, FL, and the one time legal guardian of William James, cornerback for the New York Giants and now the Philadelphia Eagles. He and I sparked up an immediate conversation because of me working with the Eagles in Media Relations. He told me he ran a successful business up and down the Eastern part of the country selling a chip and scratch paint filler product for vehicles. I later would learn that he was a man in different business ventures and all seemed to be successful ones.

I told him that I did a lot of business locally with dealerships and had the capability to introduce him to a lot of dealership owners in the area. Before I knew it, in one month, I also helped him to hire a new area employee, Brian Reber, to help him grow his business. Also he asked if on weekends, I could help him sell his incredible product to some Central Pennsylvania dealerships. He offered to incent me for anytime I was able to get his company into businesses. I was able to talk with several of the dealerships and most saw a value in his product. Selling benefits to companies is my life, but I put the Law of Attraction to practice, and in a strange coincidence, I walked into a side business that only looks promising.

In my lifetime, I have read hundreds of self-help books and books on positive energy and self-changing books. I think I read them to better myself and also to better understand why I may tick the way that I do. This is the greatest of all books because as you listen if you get the CD book, Byrne's words help you to absorb her message and you will start to heal in your mind. It is a miracle. The website to purchase, *The Secret* movie and book, is www.thesecret.tv or Amazon.com. If you would like to pick this book up do it right away. For those who believe her message your life can be changed, like mine was. Learning how to think positively can only be good for the mind, particularly for people struggling with depression.

If you focus on changing your life today and the way you think, you can change your brain chemistry. As you will see throughout this book, changing the way chemicals flow through your brain, can be the difference between happiness and sadness. This book talks about the term "The Law of Attraction" and how what you think about, is what you can bring to your life. Basically, everything that comes into your direction in life, you are attracting to you. That is something psychologists and quantum physicists have known for years, but Byrne found a way to market it to mankind. The book also talks about how your thoughts carry energy or a frequency, that will attract good things to you. That is powerful stuff and thinking good things about yourself cannot be bad for you anyway you look at it. If you learn to follow the practices of *The Secret* and really harness it, you can bring peace and joy into every aspect of your life. As of recent, I have told many coworkers about the book as well as family and friends and they too have commented on how the book has changed the way they look at life.

Byrne talks about, how as humans, we can control our thoughts and with thinking positively all the time you can heal your mind and spirit. You have to learn to love yourself and if you put yourself first to heal from depression, this book will teach you how to. If you can learn to persist to only thinking positive thoughts you can control your depression or any malady.

I wish I had read such a book when I was growing up because I am confident that I could have been cured a long time ago. *The Secret*, when understood, can be life transforming and no book had ever done this to me before. I was educated about quantum physics and how energy that is in our body can help us to heal mentally and physically. I am spiritual and Byrne also talks about religious aspects of how the Bible even talked about the Law of Attraction in its contents.

You can control your circumstances in life according to Byrne, purely by controlling your powerful thoughts. Since reading the book, I made changes to my thought pattern and have seen changes in my own life right away. "If you want to feel great or get rid of your depression or be happy or get out of poverty or make more money or get a new job once you learn the Law of Attraction, you can get it," says Byrne. Many people walk through their whole life not knowing where they are going. They become depressed or can have alcoholic issues and reach to drugs or have extra-marital relationships, because they are lost. Their minds are clouded and *The Secret* will help you and console you to create the life you want and desire and it can happen in only a couple of days. It will teach you the way to think that will help you to get whatever you want while here on this earth.

Byrne says, "If you think negative thoughts you will send out negative frequencies to the universe, you will only have a negative life." If you think you will only be depressed in life you always will. Any normal person, if they truly want to heal, can only think positively and in time they will chase away their depression. Once again, that is powerful. Another author, Lisa Nichols, in *The Secret* states, "Very simply the thoughts and feelings can create your life."

While reading this book also pick up *The Secret*, and collectively by reading our books you can get better if you are willing to make changes. You can become the person you fight to be every day, simply by becoming what you think about. That is almost fun and this book helped me to heal from OCD, which to me is some kind of magical miracle. I want to bring these kinds of miracles to you as you read my pages to become you again. I inspired myself to learn the most important lesson in my life and it was to learn the Law of Attraction.

Chapter 4

OCD and the Right Occupation

"The best companies assume that each individual wants to make a difference in the world and be respected. Is that a surprise."

—*Paul Ames*

In this journey called life, we all have to work to provide for the loved ones in our lives, and I've always believed that your occupation can dictate the peace that you have, or do not have, in your life. I am sure that many readers would agree. Being in the wrong job, even if you make lots of money, can take a terrible toll on your happiness and psyche. That's true for everyone, and for an OCD sufferer the disease adds another layer of difficulty to the challenge of dealing with the wrong job or with a bad boss. We have all had those bosses that have worn us out and drained us in our lives.

St. Paul Fire and Marine Insurance Company sponsored a study, and it supported the belief that job stress can lead to many of the health issues encountered by businesses. Plus, productivity is greatly affected when people work for a stressful company. I have worked for these kinds of companies where the health of employees is not a concern and morale was really low. Many hours are lost within companies daily, due to employees calling off work due to stress or exhaustion.

The stress brought on by the job brings more stress to an individual than financial and or family problems. So, to this end, people with OCD or depressive problems really have to focus on the job that they do daily. Many people believe that you have to have stress in your workplace to be successful and to show that you work hard. That could be true, but people with Obsessive Compulsive issues need to be even more aware of their jobs. Different workers cope better with stress than others. I worked with many people over the years, who went on anti-depression medication or were seeing psychologists, because they were diagnosed with severe anxiety or colitis and other health struggles because of things going on at work.

Early signs and warning signs of occupational stress includes:

- Headaches and migraines
- Obsessive crying while on the job
- Difficulty focusing
- A bad temper
- Upset stomach
- Excessive tardiness
- Low company morale
- Family problems

The National Institute of Occupational Safety and Health (NIOSH) has studied the effects of job stress and health for years. NIOSH has clearly listed some chronic health problems that arise when people are heavily stressed at their jobs. They are as listed:

- Cardiovascular disease
- Musculoskeletal condition (i.e. Sore back)
- Psychological disorders (i.e. Depression)

I, myself, love the challenge and the excitement of sales, and I've worked in sales most of my life. In addition to my sales career I currently work with the Philadelphia Eagles, just during the season in Public Relations and Media Relations. I've sold products for telecommunication companies, employee benefits companies, and insurance carriers for many years.

Let's face it, most of us work nine- to eleven-hour days and some parents spend as much time as possible with their children. When you spend that much time working at your job and rearing children, it's critical that when you have OCD, you learn to love what you do at work. Plus I have found that it is critical to take vacations and have down time to be healthy because work can be so stressful. Stress and anxiety from your work can lead to a lot of OCD incidents and I have seen it countless times in my own life and in others.

I've earned nice incomes in sales, but the price of making that money has often led to a high level of stress. A salesman is only as good as his most recent performance, so I could sell a million-dollar deal on Monday, but if I don't land anything on Tuesday, the boss will want to know what I did wrong. That's job stress. I have probably exaggerated this a bit, but salespeople would understand where I am coming from.

Salespeople have quotas and goals—meet them and you'll be successful; exceed them and you'll receive bonuses and recognition; fail to meet them and you may soon be looking for a new job. Sales professionals are the ones who drive new revenues for a company and new sales have to always be coming in for the company to grow.

A recent article by Jim Citrin, of the Yahoo Finance website, stated that the Gallup polling organization compiled results after doing workplace interviews. Citrin surmised that, "The poll found that an employee's job satisfaction is the key determinant of his happiness and his (or her) effectiveness inside that organization."

This research stated something that I found quite intriguing. It said that if you had a best friend at work, it could correlate to an individual's happiness with his or her job. The Gallup research showed that work needs to be a place of trust, nourishment, and a place where you have friends, to be satisfied with your job. If you do not have this where you work, and I am sure many people do not, you need to sit down and clearly think about your career path and what you need to do in the future.

Bosses can be tough, but the boss is never a salesman's toughest critic. Every salesman expects to close every deal, and when he doesn't close one, he can feel a sense of failure. If he doesn't close a deal for a week or a month, he can start to wonder if he'll lose his job. For a person with OCD, it's important to be able to manage these feelings if you want to stay in sales.

Most people are not fortunate enough to have the perfect job, but working with good people and for good companies can alleviate a lot of undo stress. Stress in life or in the workplace can lead to marital conflict and health problems, and, according to a study done by the *USA Today*, 75% of Americans are dissatisfied with their jobs. This is a good analysis that means work claims and loss time at work will continue to grow. That means that you have to learn to have patience and a positive attitude in order to survive in today's workplace. You need to find something that you are good at and excel in if you want to live a happy life.

For many salespeople or anybody working, their jobs involve a lot of driving to appointments, jumping on airplanes, working with difficult customers, and spending countless hours to close a sale.

New sales drive a company, and without new sales most companies cannot survive and flourish. So, as a salesman with high expectations, I've had many times in my life when I've had to put the company ahead of my mental well-being. For doing so, I've often paid a painful emotional and physical price. Job-related stress can trigger bouts with OCD, and I know that stress led to many of mine. You do not have to be in sales to feel stress because all kinds of jobs have their own kinds of stress.

One particular incident stands out above all the others that happened to me while I was working for a certain company. When it occurred, my OCD became so bad that I truly believed that I was going to die. This incident was terrible when it happened, but it turned out to be a good thing for me because it motivated me to get myself out of a job situation that was hurting my emotional health and my family. If you see yourself in my story, have the courage to put your life above your job.

Several years ago, I worked for an insurance company, and someone looking at me from the outside would have thought that I had the perfect life. I had a great income and did not pay anything for health benefits that covered my entire family and me. I also had a high car allowance. If money were all that mattered in my life, I would have had the perfect job.

I worked for this company for a little over three years, and we had an outstanding product. However, management was unreasonably demanding, and most employees felt that we were micromanaged in every facet of our jobs. Company morale was down and I was working probably close to twelve-hour days and was just flat out worn out.

Even though I had a lot of stress while I worked at this job, I think the antidepressant I took, which was Paxil, gave me balance in my life and helped to curb some of the stress. When I was with this company, there was constant pressure, fear of failure, and a fear that I could lose my job at any moment. Because stress can bring on my episodes with OCD, this was not the best place for me to work.

Management knew that many employees worked full days and then were working most nights, as well. The company's managers were completely aware of how hard we were working, but they felt that it was just a part of our job, and the welfare of their employees was not a worry to them. The company philosophy was to manage with fear.

Working in that office was a very uncomfortable situation, and when we would be in sales meetings, many of the employees would be afraid to speak out because of the way they would be perceived. Anytime a salesperson cannot be able to speak on what might make the company better is not good for the mental state of their employees.

That atmosphere created really bad company morale, and even though we were paid well, many people resigned. They were making good money, but their lives suffered terribly. We were working all the time and not spending enough quality time with our families or loved ones. For someone like me, who had OCD, a time bomb was going on in my body and it was only a matter of time before my body would cave in.

Then, something happened that would forever change my life. It helped me to look at the world in a different way, and I reflect on it often. I have a Type-A personality, and I can go and go and go. I had been working 65- to 70-hour weeks for many months and I went on a business trip to the Eastern Shore of Maryland. My assignment was to go explain a new employee benefits program to the professors at a small college.

I was four hours from the comforts of home, and I suddenly found myself feeling just flat-out exhausted. I can go and go for weeks at a time, but sometimes that approach catches up with me and my body shuts down physically and mentally. For months, I had felt unappreciated and the stresses of the job had been mounting. Still, I always kept a good frame of mind because I was making good money and all I wanted to do was succeed in my job.

I began that trip in high spirits, but then I found myself taking a lot of deep breaths and my nerves were really shaky. I vividly remember that my OCD symptoms were at a high level, and I found it hard to concentrate on anything. I was worrying about a lot of things in my life, and I simply was not feeling good inside.

On the day after I arrived on the Eastern Shore, I did a presentation on the new dental insurance plan that the employees would be offered. I had done this presentation a million times, and I was perfectly prepared for it, but it just didn't flow smoothly. I was a little disappointed in the presentation and I was getting a lot of bizarre questions because my presentation was not as clear to the employees as it had always been.

A person with OCD is hardwired to complete things to the end, but on this day I struggled with the meeting. Because the meeting didn't go well, I felt extremely dazed and confused and anxiety was at an extreme high. It appeared that my body had shut down, both physically and mentally, and I felt almost powerless to turn it back on.

I have always been known as an outgoing and energetic person, and suddenly I was a guy who couldn't focus on anything. Almost instantly my personality had changed. I became very quiet and seemingly in my own world. I was flat-out scared to death that something was seriously wrong with me, and I absolutely could not make sense of the way I was feeling. I had never felt like this before and was really scared.

After the meeting, I went out to lunch with the college's Human Resources Director and some others with whom I had been working. Many of them noticed a complete change in my personality, and they kept asking if I was all right or if something was bothering me. An associate of mine, Serrie LaTorre-Krash, pulled me aside in the restaurant and told me she was really concerned for me and asked if I needed help.

I just smiled and told them that I was fine, but they saw the change in me and, out of concern, continued to ask me questions to try to come to terms with my feelings. Everyone was trying to include me in the conversation because the 180° change in my personality had made them uncomfortable, but I simply was not talking with anyone. Believe me when I tell you how rare that is for me to not have energy and to be quiet.

Inside, I was scared to death. I could barely form words, and my face was flushed. I was frightened and I just did not feel like myself and had not ever felt like that before.

I was having an OCD episode like no other that I had ever had in my life, and I felt as though I had no control over my thoughts and feelings. Anyone who has ever had an OCD episode like this will understand.

The combination of working so many hours, being so frustrated with the company, and having OCD had the effect of mixing oil and water together. So, my body finally said, "Ok. I'm shutting down now—deal with it."

My drive home was awful. I drove four hours home and could barely focus on anything. My anxiety was so bad that my hands and legs were shaking most of the way. I thought that if a policeman would pull me over, he might think I was either on drugs or on some sort of foreign substance because I was so wiped out.

Somehow, I made it home, but as I came into the house, I had tears in my eyes. My wife saw me and was immediately as concerned as I had seen her in a long time. I told her that I was not feeling well at all, that my heart was racing, and that I really felt as though I was going to die. I remember sitting on the front step with her watching our kids play in the front yard, wondering if I should go to the hospital or if I may die.

She wanted to get me to the hospital, but I told her that I just needed some down time. As I lay in bed, I had a fear that I might not wake up the next morning, and I was scared to go to sleep.

Eventually, I did go to sleep because I was so tired. I also woke up the next day, but the feelings that I had in Maryland were still with me in Pennsylvania, and they lasted for a couple of days. I continued to work because I refused to let those crazy feelings beat me and because my job demanded it, but I was truly struggling.

Two weeks later I reached my emotional limit. I told my wife that I could not continue to follow my crazy lifestyle, no matter what kind of money I was making. I told her that if I continued to live like that, I feared that it would kill me. My body was telling me that with my OCD, I had to make changes or it might really shut down for good. So, I made a career change a week later. That change has been great for me and for my family.

I also made some huge changes in my life after resigning from the insurance company where I worked. I made sure as always that I stayed on my Paxil and also started my regimen of taking Omega-3 fatty acids on a daily basis. As I will mention later, continued research is showing that people who are depressed may have low levels of Omega-3 fatty acids in their bodies. I also started to workout 3 or 4 days a week, during lunch breaks, which helps me to have a more positive outlook on the day and to raise the serotonin and dopamine levels in my brain.

I also changed my diet, and more and more research is showing that eating the right foods may help with depression. I started to eat more fish like tuna and shark and fruits like bananas. These foods have a lot of Vitamin B in them, and this vitamin has shown to relieve some forms of depression.

Some other foods that are good sources of Vitamin B are broccoli, cauliflower, poultry, meat and potatoes, and mangoes. All of these changes have enabled me to live a much happier life. In some later chapters I will go into depth about great supplements and foods one can eat to raise the good chemicals in your brain.

Today I still work in insurance sales, but now I work for a great company called RJP Associates, Inc. in Hunt Valley,

Maryland, as an employee benefits consultant. This is a company where management truly cares about and respects all employees who work for them. The days of micromanaging and not caring about the well-being of employees have gone away, and I enjoy my work and my life again, like never before.

The lesson from my job change is a simple one. Your life will suffer if you're miserable in your job. Having OCD or depression will make a bad job situation even harder to bear. So find a company that expects you to work hard, play hard, and live for your family. After all, if you're rich and miserable, you're still miserable if you work in a job that does not satisfy you.

I've found a job with a positive atmosphere, and that's vital. I still make a nice income and support my family, and I enjoy life again. I knew that things were really going right when I went for a doctor's visit and had my blood pressure checked. The pressure was the lowest it had been since I was in high school. Numbers can tell it all and when a guy who is 235 pounds has a blood pressure of 110/60, things are going well.

Recently, as I was writing this book and preparing to go on vacation to the shore, I received an email from my boss, Lynne. It read, "Dave, you are doing very well. Try to remember that life is short and you need to devote as much time to good mental health and family as you do to business."

Let's just say that it had been a long time since an employer had said something like that to me, and it made me feel that I had found the right place to work. I share these stories with you because I know that all people with OCD have their own stories of times when they knew that something was not functioning right in their minds; times when they knew that something inside them was wrong.

I've also shared my experiences because I want others to know that they are not alone in their fears and anxieties concerning OCD in their workplaces. The career that you choose can dictate your satisfaction with your life and help to make your relationships more satisfying and friendships with family members and people so much nicer.

 Please consider this chapter and my job-related experiences as something important when you evaluate your life and what is really important for your mental well-being. Making money is important, but not so important that you should trade in your peace of mind.

 Your job is something that you do every day, and my advice is that if you suffer from depression, find an occupation that will drive you and energize you, not one that will destroy you mentally and physically. Your mental well-being will benefit from meeting challenges, it will suffer in a negative atmosphere.

 You deserve a good boss and a positive workplace. If you don't have them now, do your best to find them. That's what I've done, and it's been a vital step in controlling my OCD.

Chapter 5

Optimism and Living with a Positive Attitude

"Optimism is the one quality more associated with success and happiness than any other."

—Brian Tracy

"We are all the captains of our own ship. We can either sink with the ship, or crash through the waves and steer the boat into a sunny port."

—Dave White

Most of my life I have been an optimist at heart, even though I had OCD. At times, I was sad but I always tried to look at life as an optimist and appreciate that God gave me the life that He did. As mentioned earlier in the book, my optimism is at an all-time high now because of reading and training with the Law of Attraction from the great book *The Secret*. At 38 years of age I am probably more happy at this time in my life than anytime in my good life. Through it all, so many people told me that I enjoyed the little things in life. Living with a positive frame of mind, in my opinion, is the way we should all lead our lives. With a positive attitude, you will accomplish so much more and your energy will make people want to be around you. That is why when I learned about the Law of Attraction and its ways, I believed its words and changed my life and the things that I did in my life. I also read books by great authors like Jon Gordon, who wrote *The Energy Addict*, about energy and maintaining it in a positive manner.

I fought with my OCD, but always remained optimistic that things would some day take a turn for the better. Later in life, I was paid back by living a great life with a great family and friends and working for a great company. Now that I have healed, I still live by these virtues today. Many studies have been done that show people who have a great outlook on life are more healthy physically and mentally. Life is like a car in that if the car is taken care of inside it will run for a really long time.

By a great outlook, I do not mean being a phony and always appearing to be happy, but being truly happy with your life. You have to feel it in your mind and in your thoughts. It means that you want to wake up in the morning and conquer life even when it brings some tough times your way. We are all going to have tough times and challenges in our lives, and that is just a part of living. You have to truly and genuinely feel happiness, purpose, and satisfaction in your actions in your gut. You have to feel it all the way to the core of your soul.

We are living in a society of many pessimists unfortunately and what we have are people around who author Jon Gordon calls "Energy Vampires,"—people who only care their own well-being and not for anyone else's. Everyone, it appears, is out to see what is in it for himself or herself. Everyone, including myself, has a bit of selfishness at times because we are all human. You have to realize that there are so many special and caring people out there though who love others and would take the shirts off their backs for someone else. I have a wife who is like that and it is so refreshing to have people like her around me.

If you want to be gloomy, it's easy to find excuses for it. Our country is at war in countries such as Afghanistan and Iraq and Iran, and some people are struggling with gas prices, with the general economy, their jobs, and other things.

You turn on the news or read website news stories and it is not hard to become easily depressed these days.

As I write this book, we are honoring our fallen heroes and the brave Americans who lost their lives on 9/11. It is the fifth-year anniversary since terrorists bombed our World Trade Centers and killed more than 2,000 beloved Americans. This has brought a lot of stress to not only the family members, but to Americans across this country. Staying positive is not always easy, particularly if you are suffering depression, but fight through it if possible.

Some begin to wonder if we are as safe as we always thought that we were. It is so easy to be pessimistic, but continued years of that attitude could kill you or lead you to be extremely depressed. And anyway, what's the point of living life like that, because life is tough enough even with a positive outlook. For people fighting depression, a positive attitude is a must because it can raise the serotonin and other neurotransmitters in the brain and that is good for all.

According to ABC reporter Pallas Hupe', a new study found that the most optimistic people have a 50 percent lower risk of dying from cardiovascular events such as heart attacks or stroke. If this is not a strong enough reason to live a pleasant life, I do not know what is.

Optimistic people also tend to have less stress, and stress is what can bring on bouts of depression, alcoholism, and OCD. "Exercise, a positive attitude, and even things like laughter can promote better blood circulation, and in turn good heart health, says Hupe'. I have also read some studies that show that an hour of exercise and a positive attitude can add an extra two hours of life each time you do so.

Smiling alone is one simple way in which someone can start off on the road to becoming an optimist. Heck, it is easy enough to do that. Studies have shown that 16 muscles are used when you smile. So if you workout at the gym to build muscles, why not lift and run on a treadmill and smile once in a while. Then watch your facial muscles grow. A sincere and bright smile can raise the happy hormone, serotonin, a word that the OCD sufferer has heard over and over.

Jon Gordon talks about this in his wonderful book, *The 10-Minute Energy Solution*. Gordon mentions Professor Paul Ekman, of the University of California-San Francisco, who did research on how all humans express the same emotions and that these emotions create certain facial expressions.

Ekman's research talks about how a smile on a person's face can change her own physiology and emotions. A smile can bond us all together and it is so easy. So my advice is to try it —it cannot hurt and it almost certainly will help you feel better. Plus, people love to talk and spark up conversations with people who seem happy and genuine.

I have always been a guy who has reached for the stars and wanted to be some kind of a rain maker. I was dealt some tough cards in my youth but I always had a nice home and loving family members around me, and I have led a great life. I have been able to be a sports writer for the *Sun Sentinel* in Miami, work for two NFL teams, and even write this book because I am positive about my life and have good feelings about my future.

My positive outlook on life probably got me through many of the tough days I had with OCD. I do realize that some do not come from great upbringings and from people who loved them, like I did. What that means is that you have some more hard roads ahead in your life to find that. But you can do it. You can always find people around you who can give love and love to receive it. All of us, at different times in our life, have succeeded at being great at something—as a parent, a musician, an athlete, an artist, or whatever. Many live here in the United States, which is the land of opportunity and prosperity, and where you can accomplish whatever you want, no matter your gender or creed. Not every country in the world can say that.

So from this day forward, why not go after your dreams, instead of being a tiring pessimist? A positive optimist will take life in stride, and if you fail in something you will learn from it and allow another positive thing to occur in your life.

Many of the people with whom I have worked have always said that they cannot believe the energy I have and the smile I have on my face almost all of the time. Luckily for me, this has not been a fake attitude, but something that I have carried with me my whole life. This is something I can attribute to my own mother. She had her bumps in the road but she always taught me how to love life. I have always had a fine sense of humor and have tried to find the best in life.

When I lived in sunny South Florida in the early 1990's, I worked in community relations for the Florida Panthers during their inaugural season. I have worked for the Washington Redskins and still work today with the Philadelphia Eagles, as a full-time seasonal employee. Since working in and around football has been my passion my whole life, I have always found a way to work in it in some capacity. When you work in an industry that is your passion, it fulfills your life and gives you a reason to want to conquer life. My bosses with the Eagles always joke with me because I have a positive attitude and they are surprised I can keep that up all the time. I love working for the Eagles' organization because the NFL has been such a huge part of my life and when I am around it I feel like a million dollars.

I worked for large companies such as MCI Telecommunications, Delta Dental, and for the Marriott Corporation in sales and service, and I have always been able to provide for my family. My optimism and zest for life allowed me to do a lot of things in my life. I think that without living positively and looking for the good in life, I would not have been able to work for the great companies I have. People when hiring, always like to work with people who can give a company a better morale.

Companies want people around who will make it a fun place to work for all. It really does not matter who the company is.

We all are writing our own chapters of our lives, and we need to learn to pat ourselves on the back once in a while for all we have done. When you get older and look at your life you want to be able to look back and realize that you lived life and had fun with the people around you. Once you have healed from your depression and/or OCD, go after life because, as you know, opportunities will not just knock at your door.

Once I felt better from my symptoms of OCD, I took the attitude that since I lost some time in life, I was going to accomplish a lot. I had to find ways to succeed in life, even with OCD, and you can too if you really want it.

As a part of life, work hard but learn to sit back and relax sometimes and take an inventory of how life is going. Spend quality time with your family and go on trips and spend great times with your family or significant others. Learn to get out and smell the clean air. Lie on a beach and close your eyes and listen to those waves crash. I have done this for over twenty years in Avalon, New Jersey, which is the beach where I go to cleanse my soul and evaluate life. We all need to have a place of peace and serenity where we can think about life and the things that we want to accomplish.

If you have a boat or a jet ski, take it to a lake, river, or a bay. Watch the fish jump, and become one with nature. Look up at the shining sun and the birds on the banks and just take it in. Go on vacation (I suggest the Florida Keys) and see a world that you have never seen. If you love motorcycles hit the road often and ride and see parts of this great country you have never been to before. If you have a hobby, get engrossed in doing it and forget about the stresses of your life. People in life sometimes like to be moving all the time and do not take the time to slow down and think about their great lives.

If you see a pretty woman or a handsome man or a nice

person, tell them you love the way they look and live life. After all, who hates compliments? It is so fun to see a smile come up on a person's face when you let them know they are a nice person or that someone is attractive.

Learn to be a great parent and love your babies because they are a piece of you. Excel in sports, music, acting, working in human services, or whatever is your passion. Always remember that when your life ends they will bury you in front of loved ones, and you'll be in the ground for a very long time. Leave a lasting legacy so that people will talk about you years after you leave this world.

I can be an example to you, in that I had OCD as badly as some of you may have it, and I was able to weather the storm. At times it's very hard, but you will make it. If symptoms come up, just tell yourself you have OCD and you will get through it. You may be depressed or really struggling in life, but be your own captain of your beautiful and sturdy ship and sail the beautiful waters of life. Either you can sink the ship or drive the boat through the turbulent waves and sail into the sunny port, called life. It is only you who can live the life you really want.

Chapter 6

Regular Doctor Appointments

"Heaven never helps the man who will not act."
—Sophocles

Because of the many years I have worked in Employee Benefits for health carriers, I have realized so much about the importance of good physical and mental health. At work and at play, unfortunately, I have seen many people struggle with drug addictions and serious medical issues, and seeing them has saddened me greatly. I have a son now and look at life differently. When I see people with drug or alcohol addictions, I realize that they are someone's son or daughter. I have written this book because I want to help those people's sons and daughters as much as I can.

One experience with a friend's depression that has had a lasting effect on me is with a guy I played in a football league with. I played on the offensive line in a football league in my hometown, and I dealth with the suicide of a popular guy who played quarterback for us. As an offensive lineman, I protected this guy, and I was with him two nights before he took his own life.

This was a guy and a teammate who really struggled with manic depression. I remember talking with him that night, asking him if he was ok, and telling him that if he needed to talk with someone, then he needed to do it—not to wait but to do it right away. I knew that he was struggling with the loss of a girlfriend, but I never dreamed he would leave this world two days later. It was my first experience of knowing someone closely and having him take his own life. He had a stubborn personality and sometimes did not take his bipolar disorder very seriously, which always concerned me.

He was diagnosed as being bipolar and committed suicide during our season. Going to his funeral still sticks in my mind. Bipolar disorder can cause a person's mood to shift from extreme depression to maniac phases where they can go through phases of being reckless, having extreme highs and very lows in their emotions, and being restless. I remember being at his funeral and seeing him lay in that casket with his football letter jacket at his side. A week before we were playing a sport we loved and the next he was gone forever. Then, within a month, his brother did the same. His brother, who also suffered from being bipolar, had two young children and a great wife, but could not deal with the death of his beloved brother. I attended both of their funerals in a three-week period, and that was an extremely sad time in my life. I bring this up to you because bipolar disorder is also a common depression in this country and the suicide rate can be so much higher than for someone with OCD. The depression these individuals can go through can be ten times the depression of a person with regular depression. Unfortunately the guy I knew was on lithium but continued to drink alcohol and live life sometimes on the wild side.

These were two good-looking guys who were both great men with great jobs. They both made great incomes, and had many good things going for them, but they chose suicide over living. I do not fault them because they were good people but it shows how serious mental health can get if not properly treated. Their depression was extreme. If you feel like that, you really have to give yourself extreme self-care all the time.

I will never forget that time in my life, and more recently some other people with whom I worked with, have chosen suicide. These men were somebody's sons. They were somebody's friends. I had an old coworker take his life after a bad breakup with a girl who he loved a lot. I just wish they had gotten the help that they needed so they would still be with us. Some of these men were in their thirties and still had so many years in their lives to accomplish so much.

According to Dr. Jose Manuel Bertolote, a mental health official at the World Health Organization in Geneva, some 20 to 60 million people try to kill themselves each year, but only about one million of them succeed. It is so scary to think that that many people would be depressed enough to even think of taking their lives. Life is so precious and we are all so lucky to have been born and should live great lives and not feel so low. If you are one who has considered suicide, do yourself a favor today and reach out to a doctor or to a friend and ask for immediate help.

Dr. Bertolote also mentions that enough people succeed yearly in killing themselves that more die every year from suicide than from war and murders. This is such a sad fact and part of the reason why I've written this book. If you can get the help you need and not wait, you can recover from depression, but you have to be the one to take action and to seek help. Do not reach to drugs or alcohol because you are just using those substances as a band-aid.

We have a national issue, and it has to become a priority to let people understand that they can get help instead of committing suicide. One group that is at particular risk for suicide is medical professionals such as dentists, doctors, and veterinarians, because they have access to lethal dosages of medications and know how to handle them. It is kind of weird when you think about it but these are professions with a lot of stress as we all know.

Over the years I've talked with a lot of friends and work associates and when they have struggled, I have not hesitated to push them to talk with a psychologist or a doctor to understand their feelings and to take steps toward feeling good again. Everyone has different times in their life when they are really down and they must know when to seek help.

In my job I've worked with many employees at local companies and at companies throughout the Mid-Atlantic region, and have had many of them tell me that they had not been to a doctor in years. Everyone should check in with a doctor yearly to get blood work done, have their blood pressure checked, and get tested to make sure they are functioning ok. Struggling mentally can effect so much in your life that it is good to see a doctor regularly just to let them know that you are doing well.

I remember being at a meeting at a manufacturing plant in Pennsylvania, when a gentleman stood up and said, "Insurance companies should pay me for the cost of insurance because I have not been to a doctor in twenty years." I looked at this disheveled gentleman, who appeared completely worn out, extremely overweight, and was missing some teeth, and thought that this was a guy who needed to see a doctor more than anyone else in the room. He definitely was not a happy person and his personal appearance showed it.

He is like a lot of men, in that they have to be half-dead before they will step through the door of a doctor's office. It has also been my experience that a lot of men have their pride and they believe that going to a psychologist or to a doctor would show weakness, but this just is not true. I really think that anyone, man or woman, suffering with health issues and or mental conditions, has an obligation to himself or herself to see a doctor yearly. If you want your body to hold up, you have to take care of yourself.

I probably look at doctor appointments and a psychologist differently than a lot of my male counterparts do because of being raised predominately by my Mom and my sister, Heather. They have always been women who made Ob-Gyn and doctor appointments regularly, and they have really taken responsibility for their self-care. I am glad I was trained to take care of myself from a young age because that training made me able to ask for help when I really needed it.

Scheduling a yearly physical to check in with a doctor is so important to maintain your optimal health. If you are working through depression or are stressed, it is particularly more important to have yourself checked. If you are taking different kinds of medication you need to check in with a doctor who may take you off medications completely or change the doses of your medication. Whenever you go to the doctor, it is good to ask for flu shots or cholesterol checks, heart evaluations, and blood panels to make sure you are functioning well. Some people are uncomfortable with doing that but you need to live a good life.

I have talked with many people with OCD and other mental conditions, who are scared and confused on how to address their situations with their doctor. I know that until I opened up with my doctor years ago, I was afraid to talk with him about my sometimes bizarre thoughts and behaviors. But thank God I did because I am a completely different person than I once was.

I was fearful that I might be institutionalized or something. Most doctors will be there for you and will understand your fears because of going through this situation with others. If your doctor does not seem to have the adequate training in mental health or is not responsive to your concerns, then seek out another doctor. We do that if we do not get great service from a store so we should do the same with a doctor. There are so many great ones out there.

As a child, I went to the doctor countless times because I was a hypochondriac and would sometimes truly believe that I had different illnesses. I had a caring doctor who understood that I had some issues with a fear of death, but OCD just was not known really well when I was growing up. Now I have a different doctor and we talk about my OCD every time I go for a checkup because we have both accepted that it is a part of my life and probably always will be.

This behavior is common among people who suffer with OCD, because they need assurance and reassurance that they are going to be all right. As I have grown, a lot of this has gone away but I do like to check in with my doctor on a regular schedule. You should be seeing your doctor at least once a year for a full physical, at the bare minimum.

As a child, I was certain that I had cancer, brain tumors, heart problems, and other illnesses and I sought constant assurance that I was ok. Doctors would check me and ask why a kid as physically fit and athletic as I was would be so preoccupied with being ill. I did not always know what to say to them. I could not always explain my actions, and sometimes the fears and anxieties from my OCD would get the best of me.

This preoccupation with my health was the thing I obsessed about most with my OCD. I would always seemingly apologize to the doctors and tell them that I did not know why I felt the way I did. Then, they would make me feel ok, until the next time I would go to see them. I sometimes hated myself for being so preoccupied with my health, but I just could not control my feelings.

As a part of your self-care, I strongly recommend to everyone that you see a doctor regularly, even though you may be feeling better if you are on medication or in therapy. Checking regularly with your doctor or psychologist will help you continue to make progress on your recovery. From this day on, if you are depressed you owe it to yourself and to your family to be checked.

Over the years, since I have not been suffering from OCD, I've noticed on checkups that my blood pressure is way down and my whole body feels great. I have forced myself to eat better and to work out regularly, and if you can combine those steps with your therapy and medication, you will continue to heal and to feel wonderful. I have made this a prerequisite for my life and as I get older and still have OCD, I will continue to check in with a doctor and psychologist and not be ashamed that this is who I am. Try it and you will never feel so good.

Chapter 7

Cognitive Behavioral Psychotherapy

"The only medicine for suffering, crime, and all other woes of mankind is wisdom."

—Thomas Huxley

"Wisdom denotes the pursing of the best ends by the best means."

—Frances Hutcheson

Cognitive Behavioral Therapy is a form of psychotherapy that emphasizes the important role of thinking in how we feel and what we do. Cognitive-behavioral therapists teach that when our brains are healthy, it is our thinking that causes us to feel and act the way we do. Therefore, if we are experiencing unwanted feelings and engaging in unwanted behaviors, it is important to identify the thinking that is causing those feelings or behaviors and to learn how to replace this thinking with thoughts that lead to more desirable reactions.

During sessions of Cognitive Behavioral Therapy, a psychologist can help a person to realize that when he is feeling good mentally, he will realize that his thinking can control the way he acts and feels. The psychologist will also work with someone with depression, to help that person realize that when he has unwanted thoughts, he can control what he is thinking so that he can feel good again. I guess that is why I have enjoyed the book *The Secret* so much because I have grown to realize that when I am thinking positively my life just seems to flow.

Many people with OCD realize that they are obsessed with troubled and horrible thoughts and that they are checking things and worrying all the time. If a person is not comfortable with taking medication daily, she can try Cognitive Behavioral Therapy first, to see if this can lessen her OCD symptoms. This is always a better way to try to tackle OCD, because the cost of the antidepressants and their side effects can be tough on many.

Many people who will confide in a loved one or a spouse or friend do not always think that a psychologist can help them. I offer my experiences as evidence of the value of talking with a mental health professional, and I strongly urge everyone with OCD to talk about it, to stop feeling fear or embarrassment, and to accept the fact that OCD is a disease. Sometimes when you can go in and talk with a professional about your thoughts the stress that can be taken from you can be insurmountable.

Depending on the severity of your depression, sessions with a training practitioner may help you to heal. Without outside help, a cure is almost impossible when depression has taken over your life. So, talking with a family member or loved one can be the important first step in admitting to yourself that you are hurting inside and need some help.

Talking with a loved one, spouse, or friend can also be highly valuable because it can lead to learning how to talk with a therapist. Then if the therapy does not work, the OCD sufferer can consider being put on medication, if that is needed. The most important step is to admit that you need help and then to let a doctor help you.

Everyone's makeup is different. Everyone has had different circumstances that have brought on OCD episodes, so what might be best for one might not be so good for another. Whether it is Behavioral Therapy or medication, as long as the OCD symptoms get better, that is the most important thing.

When you are in therapy, sit back, relax, and free your mind. Some psychologists even talk with their patients about getting involved in meditation or yoga, to help one become at peace with their mind. Make sure that you allow yourself to completely trust someone else and then open up and let the psychologist know each and every thing that is bothering you. He or she cannot properly diagnose you if he is not completely clear on the way your mind is operating.

I would tell anyone that therapy would always be the better alternative to medications because of some of the side effects of SSRIs. I was one who went on Paxil because for me my brain needed it. But, as I expressed before, I am not a doctor or psychiatrist, and those kinds of decisions should be left to trained professionals.

When I was younger, my therapist used psychotherapy on me at different times. It allowed me to talk comfortably about my different, conflicting feelings. When I was not comfortable talking about my OCD with family and friends, I was able to confide in my therapist. After all, sometimes opening up to a stranger can be more easy than talking with judgmental family members. Plus some of us might not have family members or friends who are concerned with our well-being. My psychologist worked hard with me in therapy, to teach me to replace my unhealthy thoughts with positive and good thoughts. This really helped me through some tough times when my OCD was really troubling to me.

I felt that some of my thoughts were a little crazy and weird, and those thoughts and concerns were not the easiest things to talk about with the people closest to me. I was always comforted when I would ask my therapist if he dealt with people who thought like I did, and he would say that of course he did. That would allow me to realize that I was not the only one fighting this battle in my life. Sometimes when you are depressed, you look around at others and they seem to be living normal lives, and you feel you are the only one stricken with OCD. You wonder why everyone else seems to be getting on with life and you are being held back. Trust me when I tell you that many of these same people are going through exactly what you might.

I know that when I was able to talk to a trained professional about my scary feelings, I was always comforted that I could tell someone about my fears without being judged. He would then work with me, using psychotherapy, to help me learn to control my thoughts so that I could control my actions and behaviors.

I remember that during some of my sessions, I would sincerely feel that I was dying of cancer or some form of a brain tumor because I feared death so much. My therapist explained that I was a hypochondriac and that I was too young to be obsessing about my health. When I started to tell myself a lot that I was healthy and young and not to always think those thoughts I would seem to feel so much better inside.

He worked with me to help me understand that I had been to the doctor frequently, that I was in perfect health, and that I had to help my brain understand that fact. Under my breath, I would repeatedly tell myself that I was healthy and that I would be ok. By saying that over and over I had conditioned myself to believe that I was going to be alright. Once I said that enough, I would seem to feel better. If you tell your brain something enough, it starts to think that way. Remember that like attracts like.

One part of my brain would be saying that I was an athlete and that I was fit and "Why do I have to waste my life obsessing about being ill?" Another part of my brain would keep thinking that maybe I was dying and that I should be reassured that I was not. I loved who I was and respected myself, but why I continually beat myself up mentally was something that I never understood. My therapist helped me to understand why

I was acting the way I was, and that understanding brought me comfort.

Bruce, my psychologist, was something of a father figure to me because I was not close with my own father while I was growing up. My father was an executive with Libby McNeil Foods, and sometimes I did not feel like a priority to him. I truly believe that feeling was part of the reason that I developed OCD and had some of the emotions that I had in my youth. I learned to trust this other man, my psychologist, to direct me on how I was going to get better. A son's relationship with his father and mother is so important in his formative years and I did not always have that with my own Dad. My Mom went out and found a psychologist in Bruce, who cared so much about my well-being. He and I are still friends today because although I was not his son, he treated me like I was.

I also found out later in life that some of my OCD was hereditary because other members of my family had had it. Many studies have shown that OCD is indeed hereditary and it might not be a situation in your life that brings it on.

I saw my psychologist on and off for a couple of years, and he worked with me to train my brain to think good things and to try to enjoy growing up. During psychotherapy, Bruce would allow me to open up comfortably on what angered me and what scared me to death, and he taught me to change the way I was thinking. I continued to do this while I was in high school and college and it helped me to really grow up as a person.

I think that listening and doing what he asked me to do allowed me to feel like I had control of my thoughts a lot of the time. Having this control allowed me to heal in some respects.

Because of his experience in working with children, he was able to assess my thoughts and carefully try to bring resolutions to them every time I went to see him. He would continually assure me that my feelings were normal most of the time, and this reassurance helped me to build my self-esteem and my outlook on life. So for me, psychotherapy was a life-saving event for me at different times in my life.

His office was always a haven of peace for me in a time when I needed a friend just as much as a doctor. We still talk once in a while and I still thank him for caring enough to help me and to get me through therapy and later put me on Paxil. I still consider him a great friend and someone who helped make me the man that I am today.

Psychotherapy is something which, in my opinion, all people with OCD should consider, because for a long time you think you can beat OCD on your own, but sometimes you just cannot. Asking for help takes a lot of guts, and at first opening up to someone else might be the hardest thing you ever do, but you will benefit from it. Trust me.

If the therapy does not work for you, a therapist can always talk with your physician to see if medication should be the next step towards your recovery, or if another treatment may be beneficial. Psychotherapy really helped me grow, but medication as I mentioned before, was something I later needed. I look back on my sessions with Bruce and I can remember walking out so many nights feeling like I was growing up and that I was normal even though I was still working through my OCD.

Chapter 8

Paxil and Other SSRIs (Selective Serotonin Reuptake Inhibitors)

"Fortify yourself with contentment, for this is an impregnable fortress."

—*Epictetus*

Paxil or paroxetine, is the prescription drug that got me back on the track to recovery from my OCD. Paxil has definitely changed my life for the better. Many medications are available to people suffering from depression, and Paxil is what was prescribed for me. Paxil is great for people who suffer from such conditions as depression, OCD, social anxiety disorder, panic disorder, and post-traumatic stress. It has made me a better man and in some ways saved my life. There are many good antidepressants now out on the market and probably more today than ever.

Prozac is the name most commonly known for depression medication and was first developed by Eli Lilly almost twenty years ago. Almost 10 million people take that medication, and it has cured thousands of people with many disorders.

Paxil is a prescription drug that has garnered much media attention lately because of its potential risk of suicidal behavior in younger adults, most in children and teenagers. A study recently done with 15,000 patients using Paxil and dummy pills found that the frequency of suicide attempts was higher in young adults who were taking the prescription drug.

In October of 2004, the FDA concluded that antidepressant medications can increase the risk of suicidal thinking and behavior in children and adolescents with depression. So it is extremely important that younger children and teenagers are strictly monitored by their doctors when going on these prescriptions. During the study, there were eleven suicide attempts with the users of Paxil and none resulted in death. Reports showed that eight of the people tested, were between the ages of 18-30 years.

Also, there was some recent news that came out about Paxil and it said that the drug could cause a "hostility event" in some who took the antidepressant. I have also seen studies that said if you went off the drug abruptly this could occur.

A study was done, and it found that 60 out of 9,219 people who took Paxil, or 0.65 percent, had this "hostility event" compared to 20 of 6,455 who were given a placebo, or 0.31 percent. It should be noted that all the patients who participated in this study had major depression or some serious psychiatric disorders.

With anything, there are risks involved, and I can say that for me, Paxil has done wonders. It also really shows the importance of continuing to be evaluated by a doctor after going on any antidepressant. Some of the side effects of Paxil include nausea, diarrhea, constipation, decreased appetite, and some sexual side effects. Luckily for me I have not had any of these side effects, but all individuals are different. If someone ever went off the drug abruptly they could have some anxiety, abnormal dreams, mood fluctuations, and headaches. You should slowly go off the drug only if your doctor feels you could go off your antidepressant. If you go on www.webmd.com all the side effects are clearly listed for its users.

There are also some studies according to John Gray, Ph.D., author of *Men are from Mars and Women are from Venus*, that are coming out that say SSRIs can be bad for some people.

Gray has said that cortisol levels in the body can increase and that can raise sugar levels in the body and also slow down the immune system. He has also said that SSRIs can cause the brain to stop naturally making its own serotonin and this could really hurt someone if they ever went off the medication. So with studies out like these, I think this should be addressed with your doctor before going on any SSRI.

Contradicting the recent fear of Paxil is a new study that showed some positive attributes of Paxil and other SSRIs. According to Dr. Wanda Filer, who is a well-respected doctor and health reporter in Central Pennsylvania, a new study showed that before 1988, when SSRIs showed up on the market, there was a steady level of suicide in the United States.

But, with the evolution of SSRIs, there has been a big decline in suicide rates in the United States since the late 1980's. Dr. Filer mentioned that as many as 33,000 people's lives have been saved from suicide because of antidepressant drugs such as Paxil, Zoloft, and others. Reports say that new labeling may be coming to these drugs. These new labels will have warnings of the risk of taking some of these medications.

Dr. John E. Karns, the director of clinical development for Glaxo-Smith Kline, the maker of some depression medications, still says that the drug benefits outweigh the risks.

I was prescribed Paxil on that day I entered my doctor's office, and to this day I attribute most of my recovery to Paxil. I am one of the people who have seen some great things happen to their life with SSRIs. I was not suffering from major depression, and even though OCD was a tough journey for me, suicidal thoughts never crossed my mind. I just needed a drug that would cut down on my anxiety and take the edge off.

Still, my OCD symptoms were strong, and Paxil has helped me to move past them. Literally within a couple of months of being prescribed Paxil, my OCD symptoms decreased tremendously.

We all have to remember that everyone has different degrees of OCD so it may take longer for some to heal from OCD than others. Some have mild disorders and obsessions, and some are seriously depressed with high degrees of obsessions and rituals. I have talked with several doctors and there is a chance that I may have to be on the drug for the rest of my life. I have never been so happy because my chemical imbalance has been regulated, so I could very much live with that.

Paxil and Paxil CR (Controlled Release Tablets) are antidepressant medications that are prescribed regularly to patients for mood disorders and depression. These antidepressants are members of the selective serotonin reuptake inhibitors family, and were approved for treatment of OCD in 1996. Paxil CR is the newest of the prescriptions. It is slowly released into the body for continuous relief as it is taken during the day.

I would be remiss if I did not list some of the possible prescriptions like Paxil and some of the other SSRIs, such as Zoloft, Effesor XR, Wellbuetrin, Prozac, and Celexa. These medications work for different kinds of depression and depending on what you are troubled with will dictate the prescription your doctor might put you on.

Stephen G. Bloom, a professor at the University of Iowa, did some continued studies that mentioned that some of these antidepressants could clobber sex drives in up to 60% of those who take them. I have had some issues with this but they were mild. Bloom mentions that many OCD sufferers will accept their change in libido or sexual drive for a while to feel peace and serenity in their lives again.

The problem that some associate with the lack of sex drive is that the neurotransmitter dopamine, known to increase one's sexual drive, can be suppressed. Some people, when taking SSRIs, can have problems ejaculating or having orgasms.

In addition, in 2006 the FDA sent out a warning for Paxil users that babies born to women who took the drug during their first 12 weeks of pregnancy could possibly suffer birth defects. Glaxo-Smith Kline did a study with 3,581 pregnant women and found that 4 in 100 women who took Paxil or Paxil CR, during the first twelve weeks of pregnancy had babies with birth defects. Other studies showed that pregnant women who took other antidepressants had 2 in 100 babies born with some form of birth defect. There are some risks with taking SSRIs, but it was a chance I wanted to take.

These SSRIs work by allowing the brain to utilize the available levels of the neurotransmitter serotonin more efficiently. Neurotransmitters help with the brain's function and control of the thoughts we think and many other functions. Neurotransmitters are hormone-like chemicals and they can help control our nervous system and the entire body. These chemicals can help the way we feel as well as stimulate thoughts and our memories.

A low level of serotonin and dopamine utilization is considered one of the causes of depression. In turn, anxiety disorders can lead to low levels of serotonin because serotonin is necessary to metabolize the hormones created by stress. If you take anything out of this book, it should be that learning to regulate your brain chemistry with the chemicals like serotonin (contentment and mood), dopamine (motivation and readiness), and norepinephrine (alertness and concentration), and how we control these neurotransmitters can dictate your whole life.

So, low levels of serotonin can cause depression, and depression can cause high levels of stress. SSRIs help the body maintain a healthy level of serotonin and neurotransmitters. SSRIs help regulate a person's mood and attitude and help you to maintain a good outlook on life. Later I will touch on some great foods and supplements that can help to raise the serotonin and dopamine levels in your brain. I have changed my diet to make sure that these foods and vitamins are a huge part of what I consume.

John Gray, Ph.D., has sold over 40,000,000 copies of the book *Men are from Mars and Women are from Venus*, which is unbelievable. He also has a new book out on the market called *The Mars and Venus Diet and Exercise Solution* and it goes into great foods and supplements and exercises one can do to cleanse the toxins in their bodies and spur dopamine and serotonin. Gray has a superb website at www.marsvenus.com and he is a man who has helped thousands of men and women understand the difference between the sexes. He is also extremely knowledgeable about the functions of the brain and how the chemicals like dopamine in men and more serotonin in women's brains, can control their moods and behaviors.

I found it so interesting on how he says that women are planners and organizers of many families and how they can deplete their serotonin so much during the day which explains why they are so tired at night. Gray also talks about the minerals of the brain and how chemicals like lithium can be increased, to help promote the production of serotonin. After studying Gray he has enabled me to become so wise on what I can do and talk with others to be more healthy. I really respect this man so much and will continue to frequent his website and read his books on what I can do to fight depression.

SSRIs can help to greatly reduce depression and anxiety and are something that I wish I had had in high school and college. I would have been able to feel great and not have worried about all that I did.

Recently I was on a flight to Dallas, Texas, and I got into a conversation with one of the stewardesses about antidepressants and her son. She talked with me for a while about her son and his struggles with antidepressants and manic depression. She was extremely concerned with his well-being because she loved him so much.

She told me that her son seemed to do so well while he was on medication and then would drop very low when off the medication. He was like a lot of people, in that they like to go on and off their medication, but you can relapse so quickly if you do this without consulting a physician.

I cautioned her that I had talked with several people over the last few months just on that subject and that he had better get help and talk with his psychiatrist or doctor immediately. She told me that over the years when he was off his medicine, he would mention about not wanting to live anymore and have thoughts of suicide. This is very common for people who go off their medications while they were still combating depression. I commented to her that she needed to remember, "That you cannot force a horse to the trough and that if the horse does not drink the water he will die in the sun." Her son needed to reach down deep and realize that he needed help and because he was in his thirties, he needed to be the one to reach out for help.

I told her that he needed to continue to fight his depression and be mature enough to get the help he needed. We are all accountable for our bodies and our minds, and going on and off antidepressants can be deadly in my opinion.

Even though I was troubled with OCD in my youth, I was still able to accomplish so much. In junior high school and in high school I played soccer, basketball, and baseball and was able all through college to get good grades. I was able to conjure up the concentration I needed to focus on my school work and on sports. So, even though you have OCD you can accomplish much, and for me, being on the proper medication saved my life.

In conclusion, some SSRIs will greatly help people to beat their OCD and other forms of depression and to change their lives. Paxil did that for me, and I may have to be on the medication for the rest of my life, but I am ok with that. I would never want to have a relapse and feel the way I did for many years of my life.

The SSRIs help with your chemical imbalances in the

brain and for some if they go off the antidepressants they can have relapses. I will check in with my doctors yearly and make sure that they are comfortable with me staying on Paxil. Plus depending on the stresses in your life they can either lower your dosages or raise them as need be.

For some of you, however, it might be in your best interest to go through psychotherapy or other forms of counseling to help you feel whole again. I truly think that for my OCD I need Paxil and the rise in serotonin levels in my brain, to help me function and feel the way I need to feel. I have felt more stable with my OCD after taking the medication and for that I owe my recovery to the medication Paxil.

Chapter 9

The Essential of a Proper Diet

"Happiness resides not in possessions and not in gold; the feeling of happiness dwells in the soul."
—*Democritus*

Over the years, as we age, a proper diet can be so important to our mental and physical well-being. The different foods and vitamins that you take can help you to be more happy and live longer lives. Beverly Clevidence, Ph.D., U.S. Department of Agriculture, Agricultural Research Service, talks about "super food" and says that you "need to think about color when you eat food." She is a research leader at the USDA's Diet and Human Performance Laboratory.

Clevidence says that foods that are deep blue, purple, red, yellow, green, or orange are the foods that you should always consider eating. The carotenoids and anthocyanins, that provide the color for these foods contain health-enhancing nutrients that can protect your heart and fight cancer, and "can improve someone's sense of balance, our memory, and other cognitive skills." A proper diet, in my opinion, is extremely valuable to someone who is suffering any form of depression.

Interesting studies have shown that when women are depressed, a lot of the time their levels of serotonin are low. While for men the brain chemical dopamine, which gives them energy and will in life, is low. Eating some healthy foods can help both of the sexes to be more mentally healthy in life.

In particular, foods that are deep blue, purple, and red,

such as blueberries, eggplant, strawberries, raspberries, cherries, aloe vera juice, and lemons to name but a few, can lower the risks of heart disease and help with liver function and, most importantly, help with mental functioning.

Foods that are rich in protein can help raise the levels of serotonin and dopamine in the brain. This can be good for people who want alertness, thinking power, and a positive outlook on life. A good serving of fish, red meat, chicken, turkey, and eggs can help boost dopamine and another neurotransmitter norepinephrine, which is great for the body. Beans and legumes and even coffee, milk, and green tea, can help speed up these neurotransmitters in your brain. Also herbs like ginseng, dandelion, and peppermint raise dopamine levels and this is really important for men in particular.

Flavonoids are chemicals found in a person's bloodstream and are found in a lot of bright berries. A healthful flavonoid is Quercetin. Fruits such as loganberries, cranberries, blueberries (my favorite), goji berries, acai berries, bilberries, and black currant are some of the berries that have Quercetin in them. These are great berries that contain a lot of fiber and Vitamin C, which help to fight cancer and heart disease and many other conditions.

These berries are best when frozen, to keep the antioxidants in them, and can be added to smoothies and power workout shakes. I love to have these smoothies during the day and before I workout at the gym. If you are not a big berry eater make this a huge part of the change you can make to better your health.

Since I was very young I was always a pretty good eater. I was aware of my vitamins, and I made smoothies from veggies and fruits, that were packed with nutrients and minerals. In addition, I have always loved working out at a gym, and the smoothies packed with essential protein powders helped me to heal more quickly, so there were double effects to taking care of myself.

Because I was so aware of my OCD, I felt that if I were taking good care of my body, that would help me to beat my OCD. Later in the book I will talk about some scientific proof, now out on the market, of the beneficial effects of Omega-3 supplements to our diet. Omega-3 is proving to be good for the body and for brain health, and I have added this to my diet for the last five years. I have focused on eating as much organic foods as possible and I take vitamins like green tea supplements and Omega-3, and it has been astounding how great I feel.

A granola cereal that is great to try is Bear Naked Granola, and the same company also produces yogurt and other natural food products. This company makes different kinds of granola with different fruits and yogurt, and once you try them, you get hooked. It is a neat company and was started by a man and a woman who were friends and together they have built a great company. Their granola is full of things like walnuts, and some varieties contain bananas, and they are so healthy for you. Check them out at www.bearnaked.com and you will not be disappointed.

Being on a good regimen of multi-vitamins, fruits, vegetables, and grains can help cut waistlines and improve mental functioning as well. Plus, let's face it, when we are feeling more healthy and pumping minerals and good nutrients into our bodies, we are going to feel great both mentally and physically. This helps raise serotonin levels in the brain and therefore can allow one to feel less anxious or depressed.

Foods rich in whole grains including rice, oats, and corn can boost serotonin and dopamine. Other foods such as broccoli, squash, fresh fruits, and snack foods like popcorn, corn chips, nuts, and honey are also great foods to help raise serotonin.

I love to eat bananas because I remember reading about bananas as being packed with potassium and helping to raise the good chemicals in people's brains. So if you know deep in your heart that you are eating too much fast food or junk food and that your diet is not great, make a change today and stick to it. Cancer seems to also be taking so many people's lives and many of these foods and minerals are chock-full of antioxidants which can help prevent so many forms of cancer.

An exceptional dietary product I stumbled upon after studying the great Jon Gray, author of The Mars and Venus Diet&Exercise Solution, was Isagenix. Gray, who has his PHD, is someone that endorses Isagenix and this has been one of the better products I have tried in many years to enhance positive energy and loss weight at the same time. Isagenix, which is a product that can help you lose weight also has amino acids in the product that can help raise good brain chemistry. I, myself, started a regiment with the nurtrient meal replacement because you want to believe what you read. I felt great right away and was able to lose some weight right away. This powder meal replacement and snack wafers helps you to drink and or eat Amino Acids, that are digested in the stomach and absorbed by the liver.

These Amino Acids can then help produce healthy brain chemicals, which will help give you unending energy and also cut food cravings to help you lose weight. Isagenix will feed your body with aloe vera, vitamins, herbal teas, and iconic trace minerals. I have tried the vanilla and chocolate shakes and they are fabulous. You can learn more about Isagenix at www.isagenix.com and it will help you gain more mental clarity and help you gain a more positive outlook with life.

John Gray, Ph.D., on his website and in his books talks about some of the foods and chemicals that can cause some forms of depression and I found this to be very interesting. They are foods with MSG in them and also foods made with refined sugars, hydrogenated fats, and also artificial sweeteners. To my surprise, Gray talked about MSG not only being in Chinese food as people think, but that it is in most processed foods we buy in a grocery store. Gray believes that people who eat foods with these substances in it can cause serotonin and dopamine levels in the brain to be low. Gray also has said that foods with Omega-3 and foods with antioxidants in them may be in reverse good food for the brain. This in return can cause different forms of depression in men and women alike.

If you are someone who likes to drink hard alcohol and beer a lot, make a conscious effort to cut back on it. Alcohol is a depressant, and it's also a diuretic, which means that it will dehydrate you and flush nutrients out of your system.

I love my beer just as much as many but because of being on an SSRI, I have had to learn to cut back on alcohol consumption, and I can live with it. Now with having little ones I sometimes go two months without consuming any alcohol. A lot of people who are hiding their depression use alcohol to try to feel better inside. Many also turn to illegal drugs as well as alcohol, because they want to feel good. Unfortunately the high from these drugs will only last for a short time. Plus you will end up spending a great deal of money to try and feel good.

Remember, alcohol is just going to serve as a band-aid for the situation, and it will not take away your pains. Trust me when I tell you this. I had a father who died from alcoholism and I can say from experience that alcohol doesn't make the pain go away. My father was an extremely hardworking man and I really respected him, but alcoholism took him away from me.

My own doctor limited me to two drinks when I was out with friends or at a wedding. That's not always easy to do, but it is something that you have to change as you are trying to get better with OCD or depression. Because SSRIs are influencing our brain's functionality, alcohol is not going to be a good mix.

This may not be easy for a lot of people, but alcohol consumption and improper eating habits should take an immediate back seat to conquering your OCD. Your well-being and life are at stake, and I have learned that feeling good mentally is the most important thing that someone can have in life.

And, I must also admit and be blatantly honest that I am a big coffee drinker. I have been this way since I was in the eighth grade. My roommates from college would say they never needed an alarm clock because my coffee maker would always wake them up. Many healthcare professionals would tell sufferers of depression to cut back significantly on their coffee because of the amount of caffeine in coffee. The caffeine can cause someone with bad depression to become very anxious and have some serious nerves.

Because I like my coffee, what I have done is to drink café coffees, that only contain half the caffeine of some regular coffees. To be honest with you, it tastes the same as the full-blended coffees. Caffeine is a stimulant and it can make a lot of people nervous and anxious when they consume it daily and in high amounts. So, as you heal from OCD and depression, learn to cut back on coffees, sodas, teas, and some chocolates that can work against you.

According to author and health advisor Andrew Weil, studies are showing that an amino acid called L-theanine, found in tea, can help one to be more relaxed and cut down on anxiety. Some teas, particularly the herbal ones and the ones that have no caffeine are the ones to drink. L-theanine, according to Weil, is what is responsible for the unique flavor of green tea. Over the past couple of years I have made it a habit to drink teas packed with green tea and also drink the many cold teas with green tea in them.

Green tea is the most popular tea on the market today. You are seeing green tea in many drinks in convenience stores all over the country. Many people are also taking a lot of green tea supplements because of the benefits of L-theanine. Green tea may help fight cancer and lower high blood pressure but these new findings are also supporting the belief that it may help people mentally. There are just so many great reasons for adding green tea to your diet.

In the previously mentioned study, women were given two amounts of L-theanine. Some of the women were given 50 mg. and others were given 200 mg. once a week. The brain waves of the women were measured and the women who took the 200 mg. produced more alpha waves and were more relaxed than when given the lower amounts.

The results of the study were published in a June 1999 issue of *Trends in Food Science & Technology*. Green tea could be a great alternative for some coffee drinkers or it could replace coffee in the afternoon for some drinkers.

I did a lot of research as I was recovering and still stick to making sure my diet is the most important thing I do daily. I read some writings by a doctor named Michael W. Smith, M.D., and he talked about the importance of setting a schedule and trying to eat breakfast, lunch, and dinner at approximately the same time each day.

Dr. Smith said that eating on a schedule would enable a person to keep the day predictable, and he felt that eating meals at the same time every day and a couple of healthy snacks was the way to go. He believes that skipping meals and eating too late at night can end up being disastrous for many people, both physically and mentally.

Many studies over the years have shown that the recovery from and the treatment of depression can cause weight gain or loss. The medications you take can have something to do with weight fluctuations and with a person's change of attitude. If you notice this happening to you, do not necessarily hit the panic button, but do seek out your doctor for a consultation and professional evaluation.

Looking good and feeling good is something that many of us strive for every day and really desire. There is nothing wrong with that because the Good Lord only gave us one body and we owe it to Him to take care of our beautiful bodies. Limiting alcohol consumption and supplementing that with healthy juices and things like smoothies can be so important.

I have been advising this to many friends over the last year as I did much research for this book. You can kill two birds with one stone by staying fit and feeling good about the state of your physical and mental health. Just try this for a couple of weeks and I bet that you will notice the positive benefits quickly.

Chapter 10

Supplements that Can Change Your Life

"To keep the body in good health is a duty . . . otherwise we shall not be able to keep our mind strong and mind clear."

—Buddha

Besides being put on Paxil to combat my bouts of OCD four years ago, taking some supplements and vitamins and eating well have really changed my life. Numerous studies continue to show how some supplements can help with depression and OCD. Many of us know about supplements like St. John's Wort, Ginkgo, Ginseng, and B-Vitamins and the benefits associated with them. Before many antidepressants came on to the market, St. John's Wort was a powerful supplement many liked, and they still do today.

Positive reports about other supplements are surfacing on a regular basis as well, and many are feeling their great benefits.

One of the biggest changes I made in my life was to start a regular regimen of taking Omega-3 supplements three times a day (3000 iu's). I do not know if it is something mental for me or if it is really making a physical difference, but I feel awesome. Feeling so good physically has enabled me to feel good emotionally, and there are some probable explanations for this, which I want to share with you.

According to BJ Holub, a professor from the Department of Human Biology and Nutritional Sciences at the University of Guelph, Omega-3 fatty acids are polyunsaturated fatty acids, that are considered essential because they cannot be synthesized by the human body. Omega-3 is found particularly in cold ocean fish such as sardines, Alaskan salmon, mackerel, and anchovies. Omega-3 is also found in flax, canola, walnuts, and hemp, according to Holub.

Omega-3 has been known for years to benefit one's heart and cardiovascular well-being, but it seems to be doing other positive things as well. Research has shown that Omega-3 may also help a person's mental health, and I can say that it has really helped me. I have told many about the benefits of Omega-3 and they too have said that they feel mentally so much better.

These studies have shown a link between low levels of Omega-3 and major depression in people. As I studied Omega-3, I was excited to see that it is something else I can take with my medication. I talked with my own doctor, and there were no bad side effects with taking Omega-3 with an antidepressant. Now there are some cautions when taking some herbal supplements with an antidepressant so make sure you talk with your own doctor before doing so. I have made it a ritual to take Omega-3 supplements daily and have never felt better mentally myself.

DHAs (Docosahexaenoic Acids) are found in fish oil tablets. DHA levels are found to be low in alcoholics and that is because alcohol depletes DHA levels, which might be why many alcoholics are depressed. This could be an important fact that could not only help people who are depressed but also people suffering from chemical dependencies.

I remember reading something extremely interesting from a study done by the Harvard Medical School that could help pregnant women. The study suggested that women may become depressed during the postpartum period because of having low levels of DHA fatty acids. Apparently, babies in the womb crave DHA to help in the formation of their brains.

They can use a lot of the DHAs that are stored in their mothers' bodies, and this can help cause the postpartum depression some mothers have.

There are some other beneficial elements of taking Omega-3 fatty acids. Over the years, studies have shown that Omega-3 can help alleviate the pain associated with arthritis. Also, it appears that Omega-3 consumption by some mothers during their pregnancy can help with their babies' brain development, according to Joyce Nettleson, who is considered an expert on good fats.

I am fortunate to live in Pennsylvania, and to live near Burman's Natural Foods Store in Brookhaven. This store has its own Super Omega-3 supplements, which are produced exclusively for the store and molecularly distilled for supreme purity. After talking with Marty Burman, who owns the store, he cautioned me about making sure that the Omega-3 was the better distilled product than a cheaper product that could be full of mercury and other chemicals.

Whether you use their Omega-3 or other products make sure they do not contain a lot of mercury because that can be harmful to your health. The distilling process removes the PCBs, dioxins, lead, and mercury that can be found in some saltwater fish. Check out Burman's store at www.BurmansNaturalFoods.com. Marty will give you some great advice on Omega-3 and the possible benefits with brain functionality.

A study by Dr. Joseph Hibbeln, of the National Institutes of Health, has shown that higher national consumption of some fish equals lower rates of depression, in comparison to countries that consume lower amounts of fish. Areas of the world like Alaska and areas where consumption of fish is great saw less depression in their residents.

Additional research has shown that areas of the world that lower their intake of Omega-3 have seen increasing rates of depression.

I have found that consumption of Omega-3 may continue to be a huge breakthrough in helping people to deal with their depression and to feel great again. Some studies have also shown that many people suffering from depression have had low levels of Omega-3 in their bloodstreams. The way I have always looked at it has been that Omega-3 can help raise HDL levels, which is good cholesterol, in your bloodstream and, if it can help you mentally, then why not take it.

These studies are significant to individuals like you and me who are suffering from OCD and other forms of depression. Evidence of the value of Omega-3 is strong and worth discussing with a doctor. We all have different bodies and different make ups, so I would talk with your doctor before getting on a regular regimen. Some people have thicker blood and others have thinner bloodstreams so taking the right amount of Omega-3 can be important. From the bottom of my heart, I can say that with taking my Paxil daily and Omega-3, I have never felt better physically, emotionally, and mentally.

Jon Gordon also recommends walnuts and some other nuts in small handfuls. Nuts contain Vitamin E, and walnuts have Omega-3 fatty acids in them. Gordon mentions in his books that some of these nuts and fruits are great to add to shakes and to smoothies if you are a huge fan of them, as I am. This was discussed earlier in the chapter about good foods to eat to cut down on depression.

And I have saved the best news for last. In his book *Energy Addict*, Gordon also has listed dark chocolate as having chemically active compounds that can improve your mood and also help to raise serotonin levels in the brain. Dark chocolate obviously has calories in it, but like anything in life, if consumed in moderation it could help you function better mentally. And, another benefit with chocolate is that it can help you to concentrate better, and hey, we can all use that.

I have added these supplements and foods to my diet

in the last year, and the change has been extraordinary. Some supplements I have taken to control my brain chemistry have been some amino acids like folate, flax seeds, and some other trace minerals. I would be remiss if I did not mention that green tea is another great supplement that is so good for you to help lose weight and to fight illnesses such as some forms of cancer. There are many companies that are making green tea supplements that can be taken orally and they can help you to lose weight as well.

It is hard not to go to a store and see all the juices that now contain green tea and all the boxes of green tea tablets that companies are selling, so there must be some truth to this. Green tea will probably continue to be put in more products and show up on shelves and that is a good thing. Green tea and teas do contain some caffeine, if not decaf, which can give some people the energy they need during the day.

According to Nancy Schimelpfening, a woman with a B.S. degree in Biology and a M.S. degree in Community Health Education, another supplement that can benefit you against depression and anxiety is the Vitamin B complex. Mrs. Schimelpfening stated, that B1, or thiamin, is a vitamin the brain uses to convert glucose or blood sugar into fuel and that without Vitamin B, the brain runs out of energy. She says that without it, a person can feel depressed or anxious, or even have suicidal thoughts. I thank God that there are great people out there who have carried out studies like this to help educate us.

Researchers have also found that a lack of Vitamin B3 (Niacin), Vitamin B5 (Pantothenic Acid), Vitamin B6 (pyridoxine), and Vitamin B12 (cobalamin) can have negative effects on your mental functions. A popular fad right now is the energy drinks you are seeing in convenience stores and almost all of them have Vitamin B in them because it is a vitamin that is good for energy and brain functionality.

As with serotonin, a deficiency in Vitamin B can lead to mild to severe depression. The deficiency, according to Dr. Judith De Cava, Ph.D., can lead to mood swings, anxiety, vague fears, and morbid thoughts. Vitamin B-12 is stored in the liver and not always washed away like other water soluble vitamins are.

B-Vitamin supplements can be extremely important for a person's well-being. Schimelpfening, who has had personal experience with depression, emphasizes that B-Vitamins are destroyed by alcohol, refined sugars, nicotine, and caffeine. She writes for the website About.com, and you can read more from her at http://depression. She is very knowledgeable about the right vitamins you should be taking on a daily basis.

As I mentioned before, a natural supplement that has helped many people combat some forms of anxiety and different forms of depression is St. John's Wort. It is believed that St. John's Wort can naturally work like some antidepressants and inhibit serotonin reuptakes like Paxil, for some people. Always consult your doctor before taking B-Vitamins and other herbal products when on SSRIs.

And finally, Ginkgo Biloba is another herb that, according to the Wellness Directory of Minnesota, helps to increase blood circulation to the brain. It will improve memory and protect nerve cells in the body. The Wellness Directory has even gone as far as saying "Ginkgo has been shown to be a very effective antidepressant, especially for the elderly." If you have a doctor who has studied the benefits of herbs and vitamins, talk with him or her about the benefits of supplements like St. John's Wort and Ginkgo Biloba.

In conclusion, be aware every day that nutrition is vital to your well-being. You can buy many foods and supplements right over the counter that may be able to allow you to feel better emotionally. I have always been a believer in taking vitamins and eating right. I have observed that for the last couple of years, as I have really focused on giving myself extreme self-care for my OCD, taking these vitamins in conjunction with my Paxil has really helped me. I have expressed all of this in this book because I feel that I owe it to everyone with OCD, to describe my experiences in the hope that some lives can be changed. With our depression issues, we are a family, and I owe it to you to let you know what has helped me. Hopefully some of the vitamins and supplements that I have talked about can change your life.

Chapter 11

Learning to Forgive Yourself

"The more a man knows, the more he can forgive."
–Katherine the Great

Learning to forgive myself for the stresses that I had with OCD was an integral part of my recovery, so please hear this. This is such an important part of your recovery from depression because people can be hard on themselves for allowing themselves to succumb to depression.

No man or woman is perfect. If anyone says that they are, then say hello to God for me. We all have some baggage that we carry with us mentally or physically and if OCD or depression has weighed you down for years, put it behind you. We are all made the same, but some individuals just have higher self-esteem than others. Plus many people have been brought up differently and had different things that have happened to them which can affect the way they are.

As I started to come to terms with my OCD, I looked back over my life. I looked at where I had been and what plans I was going to make to move ahead. I remembered all those painful days when I beat myself up mentally, worrying about dying and fearing that I had every disease known to man. I looked back and remembered the countless hours I spent being consumed in thinking some weird thoughts in my mind.

I also felt that because of my OCD, I had lost portions of my life to worrying and obsessing about a lot of different things. I realized how the pressures of sports and the pressures of high school and being a teen and simply being a kid had affected me. I also think that the divorce of my parents had a strong impact on my life because kids lose a lot during divorce. I came from two parents who loved me but the divorce and the insecurities that come with divorce can really be tough on children. I understood why my Mom left my Dad, but the result was that I did not have that father-son relationship that is important to all men's upbringing. We all have our own experiences that shaped our lives but it is so important to put the past behind us and move forward.

I was trying desperately to get control of my life, because a kid can often feel that his life is out of control. Add OCD to the mix and you have double trouble. Many times these daily pressures would trigger an onset of OCD, with all of its obsessions and its accompanying rituals. I look back on my younger years and I am so proud of myself that I never had a drug addiction or any alcohol issues, but that was probably because I was brought up by a great mother. She loved me and taught me what was right and wrong.

I had to learn to accept the fact that I had a chemical imbalance in my brain. Admitting to myself that I had this imbalance made me realize that it was not my fault that I had OCD. That thinking helped me take a lot of heat off myself. For so long I blamed myself for the ways that I felt but I had to learn to say over and over that it was not my fault. Most of the doctors I have talked with over the years have believed that some of my upbringing could have brought on my OCD, but more likely it was heredity.

I had to understand that the imbalance caused me to obsess about little things, even though I actually had a very good life. For a person to heal from alcoholism, drug addiction, or OCD, he has to get to that day when he forgives himself. Reaching that place where you accept your condition and forgive yourself for having it is a vital step in healing from OCD.

It is vitally important that you take some time to come to terms with your depression and that you show some self-care towards yourself. Haven't we all been through enough with our OCD? You certainly won't help yourself by beating yourself up and letting past hurt feelings bring you down.

Forgiving myself was very important, but to make sure I was doing the best for myself, I also continued to see a trusted psychologist when life would get stressful. The psychologist would help me to remember how I felt when I was doing well and beating OCD.

Life will always present challenges and stresses, so it's important to avoid feeling complacent about your recovery. I faced some strong stress when I was recently separated from my wife for a couple of months, and also when we had children. These are life-altering changes, and I still talked with a psychologist about my fears during these situations because I knew that OCD could climb into my life again with stress. My wife and I worked through some issues we were having and live a great life with our beautiful and loving kids.

These events represented major changes in my life and brought on some anxiety. These are scary times in a man's and a woman's life when you get separated. It is not just about you anymore when you have children and nobody knows that anymore than me. You have people who are going to be relying on you when you are parents and I live a great life with my wife today.

I look back on these times and realize that they were events that brought on feelings of anxiety and obsessions but I got through them because of taking care of myself. When I was younger, they might have triggered bad bouts for me. Now, I've learned many steps that help me to deal with stress, and with medication and some of the changes I have made, I feel so strong inside.

During those times when I was separated and helping to raise the kids, I also realized that this was my mind and body and nobody else's, and that I owed it to myself to get the self-help that I needed. I have always stayed on my Paxil and talked with close friends or my family during stressful times in my life. Doing this is very important, so if you do not have those kinds of people around, then find them because there are so many great people in this world who will work to help you defeat depressive situations.

I am a person with OCD. This is my makeup and who I am, and I've learned to accept it and to take care of myself accordingly. This acceptance of myself and my makeup is probably why I have been able to accomplish so much in my life. I have accepted that I have something mentally that is a part of me and that I have to make sure when I am in stressful situations that I drop what I am doing and take care of my body and soul. This is probably why I also like to read a lot of self-help books and search a lot of websites on bettering myself and my life.

As a part of my healing process, I learned to accept my OCD and I was not afraid to say that I was hurting or down and needed some help. I cannot tell you how many times in my life lately something will happen and I will say to myself and to others that I have OCD, and that is why something might be bothering me. I let my closest friends and family know that I had OCD and was on medication for it and that never affected any of my relationships. They knew that I was a better man for dealing with the situation and that I had come a long way.

I hid my affliction for a long time and obviously suffered from doing that. Eventually, I could not continue to live my life that way anymore. Someone would say, "Whitey, (my nickname) do you really have OCD or are you just kidding?" I would say, "You know, unfortunately this is how I am, but hey, we all have issues of our own and this is who I am and yes I have OCD."

This exchange would often spark a conversation because the other person may have self-diagnosed himself with OCD or some form of their own depression and would ask me how they could get better. After all, many of us are depressed and if one person can take the time to care, like I have done, they too could get past their depression.

I have ended up getting into some substantial conversations with people I have known for a long time about them also having depression. Because of my research and dealing with OCD, I have given so many people advice on how I got better and on how trying some new things in life to beat depression may help them. It ends up being such a high for me to help others feel better about their life and themselves. It is one of the biggest reasons I have written this book and I only hope that the book will make its way into a lot of people's hands.

When the situation was right, I would also be compassionate with them and say to them that if they had something wrong, I would be happy to help them. I usually commented, "That I had OCD and with hard work I conquered it and they can too." Their faces would light up with a smile because they then knew someone else had what they did. I gave them hope. I want this book to help people to smile and truly feel that they are going to get better.

One of the biggest reasons I wrote this book was to encourage people to take their lives back. I want to let people with OCD know that they are not alone. I have always told people that "God knows I do not have all the answers but, I have some." If people ever wanted to talk, I assured them that I would be there. I have accomplished much in the thirty-eight years of my life, but that pales in comparison to getting through OCD, because those were some scary times in my life.

In addition to forgiving myself, I had to come to terms with something else which was my fear of God and of the person I was raised to be. I went to a Catholic school so I was raised spiritually, and religion is a powerful thing. Some people become very wrapped up in religion and fear religion when they have OCD, because they greatly fear the thoughts of the devil and hell.

As a kid I went through periods of my life when I could not curse or have anyone around me because I wanted to be perfect, so I would end up in heaven some day. Anyone that obsesses about religion probably understands how I felt. I know that at times I would really struggle with religion, and I would wonder if I was truly a good person. I love God but I had fears about the sins I would do and feared the consequences of my actions.

Over the years, I read several articles about religion and OCD being linked together. Many religious people have had OCD. They feared the devil and would obsess over even looking at the number 666 because of what it stands for. If they looked at a number like this, it could bring huge anxiety to them, just as it did to me for years when I was young. Once again, I was trying to get control of my life and I would obsess about this number and my faith.

I was raised as a strict Catholic and really desired to be a good person and to do what was right. I never liked to look at the number 6 because it represented evil and despair. Maybe some of you have had these same fears. I would sometimes look at a different number and make sure I focused on a number like a 3, 7, or 10 on a clock for instance, just so I did not have to think about a number like 6.

I would go into a video store and be unable to look at the movie covers of satanic scenes or scary pictures because crazy thoughts could cross my mind. I never understood why I would let a picture bother me, but it did. I so much just wanted to focus on the good things and scenes like this would bother me. I am past that now and have gained my own personal relationship with God as I have healed.

I think I acted like that because I was trying to control my life from something happening. I hated that so much but I think that was because I was struggling with my faith and the person who I was. We all go through times in our life when things are up and down. Today, I can look at a number such as 666 and at anything else because I am at peace with myself and my life, and because I look at God as my friend and supporter.

I vividly remember one event that may have triggered my obsession with religion. I was in high school and my parents had sent me on a religious retreat that I attended with other students from my school. During the retreat, and I think I was only about fourteen years of age, we broke off into groups with a counselor and talked about our lives and our faith.

Unfortunately for me, my counselor was a very hard-core spiritual person and he said something to the effect that all of us had committed many sins in our lives and that if we were not perfect for the rest of our lives, we would go to hell.

I was fourteen years old and insecure like most teenagers are, and he scared me to death because when you are young you are trying to figure out who you are. When someone tells you that you are a bad person and have to be perfect, that is tough.

I have since changed my religion to Episcopalian from Catholic partly because my wife is Episcopalian and because I have always thought that the Catholic religion is so strict. Especially for someone suffering from OCD, that event had a huge impact on me as I set out to lead a perfect life. Well, let's face it, that is impossible and I wish that the counselor had realized that words can scar people for a long time. Especially when the people he was talking to were young people who were trying to figure themselves out as well as life.

After that incident I watched everything that I did and said, and no one was allowed to say the Lord's name in vain around me. I drove friends nuts when I would correct them all the time. I thank God that many of them are still friends, because I was a pain in their tails.

A friend would curse and immediately I would correct him like I was a priest or something. It was my way of gaining control and befriending a God I really desired to see some day. I do not remember the retreat or even the place where I went that weekend or even who the counselor was, but his tactic of scaring a youth to death really affected me for a long time.

To this day, I remain faithful and always feel like I have a friend at my side with God. I am not a person who is extremely religious but I have my own personal relationship with God. I have learned over the last couple of years to forgive myself for beating myself up for fearing God and for ever thinking that I was a bad person. If anything, I have become an extremely caring person who sees the good in everyone.

We have all made mistakes and we will all continue to make them as we live. I have sinned as we all have, and my own personal relationship with God has only strengthened. I have learned to love God and to call upon Him when I need Him. If you believe in God, then you know He loves us all even when we are not perfect.

In conclusion, I've shared only a couple of examples of the importance of learning to forgive yourself. You may have different things that you have to let go of, but do yourself a favor and learn to do it to help yourself heal. Learning to let go is such an important step to recover from OCD and other depressions, because with the mental hiccups of OCD, you may not have allowed yourself to do this. As you are healing, learn to forgive your actions of the past and focus on growing and feeling great through self-care. You will not regret it.

Chapter 12

Read, Read, Read

"The man who can make hard things easy is the educator."

—*Ralph Waldo Emerson*

If you are struggling with OCD or some other disease, something that I found useful will also be very helpful to you. Visit a library or go online and learn as much as you can about the illness you may be suffering from. It is never good to feel constantly confused on why you are the way you are.

The more you educate yourself on your illness, the better you'll be able to understand your actions and to avoid beating yourself up mentally. This is true when you have mental conditions or any illness. Reading self-help books and magazines and self-help newsletters helped me to build awareness of my condition and continued to build my self-esteem. I think we live in a society that creates low self-esteem and people have forgotten what it is to love yourself and your mind. Take care of your mind and it will continue to take care of you.

Two websites that have been very helpful to me are: ww.webmd.com and www.ocfoundation.com. These sites talk about OCD and ways to get better. They contain some fantastic articles written by doctors and prominent psychologists. I went to the sites and typed in "OCD" and "Depression" and was able to read, read, read countless articles on OCD. After reading so much about my disease, I looked at things much differently. Right there in front of me were articles that helped me understand myself so well.

Right away I felt better because I realized that I was not the only one with OCD. I remember reading, as soon as I started searching for information, that I share the disease with eight million other Americans. I thought, "Now wait a minute. There are many other people out there like me." Mentally, it made me feel stronger to know that I was not in this by myself. I got engrossed in the many websites that the internet offers to help people with depression and Obsessive Compulsive Disorders.

I also found the website for the Obsessive Compulsive Disorder Foundation extremely informative. The compassion I saw on the page was amazing in that this foundation has such a strong desire to help others.

The foundation offers clear advice on support groups and conventions that OCD sufferers can attend. It's also possible to make contact with and talk to others who have OCD. You are able to bounce questions and your concerns off people who have what you have, and that is invaluable.

The site also has a list of psychologists and doctors in your area who can help you. There is also a glossary of OCD terms you can read to understand the definitions and terms that pertain to your disease.

If only I had access to sites like these in the 1980's, when my OCD was at its worst, they would have helped me to realize that I was not alone with OCD. Such a site might have changed my life at an early stage of my life.

The OCD Foundation's website clearly describes the so called mental hiccups that one might experience with OCD. Kudos to the OCD Foundation and other sites of its kind, for caring enough about mankind to open an informative website and to hold conferences that enable people to communicate with each other.

I am also a big fan of Barnes and Noble Bookstores. It's wonderful that you can go in there and use their free wireless internet services with your computer, get coffee, and read some books before purchasing them. I would frequent there to read whatever books I could find on OCD and I found many of them there.

For months I would go to the self-help sections and read whatever books I could find on OCD and buy some of them so that I could come to terms with myself and understand who I was. Knowledge of OCD is very important and it can cut down on so much anxiety.

I was able to continue to forgive myself because of understanding OCD and so many of the symptoms that go along with it. To this day, I continue to read self-help materials on OCD to better educate myself to talk to others about OCD and to understand myself. Understanding yourself and your actions is what can help a man or woman develop awesome self-esteem.

As I continued to educate myself, I was very touched by a couple of books on OCD that you may want to read. I read a good book about Marc Summers, who was a former host on Nickelodeon and a host of a children's show called Double Dare. He is also a national spokesman for the OCD Foundation and he wrote a wonderful book about his own trials and triumphs with OCD.

As I read the book I felt so much for this man because I had many of the same fears as he had in his life, and I really empathized with him. I was touched by his honesty and courage and for opening his life up to his readers to help others. His book is a must read.

Another wonderful book, from which I gained a ton of knowledge, was *Obsessive-Compulsive Disorders - Treating and Understanding Crippling Habits* by Steven Levenkron. Mr. Levenkron is a behavioral therapist who has worked extensively with OCD patients, and I respect him greatly for his direct experience. This is a man who has dealt first-hand with many OCD patients and in a caring way he wanted to help others understand the disease.

As I read his book, I felt as though I had my own personal

psychologist in the room with me. The book was easy to read, and because of his experience as a therapist, it was easy to trust his written words. He seemed to be a man who genuinely cared about the patients whom he treated over the years. There are many books about OCD on the market, but this book is one you should definitely add to your own library.

In an indirect way I loved the book *Energy Addict*, written by Jon Gordon, who became a good friend of mine. Jon is not an author of OCD materials, but an author who has written about maintaining energy physically, mentally, and spiritually. I read his book and was able to find ways to add positive energy to my life and see how focusing on negative energy could do to you.

Energy Addict was one of the best books I had read in years. I am an A-Type personality, and I believe Gordon's book gave me an energy kick and a positive outlook on life that is helping me to beat OCD even more. I thank God I picked up that book a couple of years ago while on a business trip. Not only did I find a new friend but I found someone who taught me how to live a fulfilling life.

Some people do not think that a book can cure a condition, but this book definitely changed the person I am today and for that I thank Jon. If you want to feel great, eat well, and learn to foster a spiritual relationship with the Lord, then read this book. Jon is an incredible writer and as you read his books you just cannot wait to get to the next page. I only hope people will feel the same way about my book.

Take advice from a past sufferer like me, that once you are diagnosed you can get better by searching the internet and reading books, along with receiving therapy.

Reading books at night and over lunch was almost like having a second job, but beating OCD has made all my reading worthwhile. It was comforting to know that others were wired like me and that there are medications I could take to change my thought patterns. The books that I read helped to make me somewhat of a specialist on depression, enough that I have been able to help others, which is a great feeling to me. I also decided one day that although I am not a psychologist, I wanted to become an expert on this disorder to help others because others had helped me.

Chapter 13

Surround Yourself Only With People Who Love You

"Lots of people want to ride with you in the limo, but what you want is someone who will take a bus with you when the limo breaks down."

—Oprah Winfrey

When writing this book, I really wanted to find a quote from Oprah Winfrey because over the last couple of years I really came to respect this woman so much. She has done some shows on OCD and depression among adults that have been so helpful for me to watch and they have helped me understand the man that I am. Her unselfishness has really astounded me because her shows have shown me how we all as human beings can love one another more. Love is paramount to our leading more productive and happy lives as we share this world together.

Oprah has shown me many examples of how people have given so much to others. Gretchen, my wife, is a huge fan of Oprah and as I would watch some shows with Gretchen, I learned to love the legacy that Oprah will leave behind.

With all the junk on TV today, it is refreshing to watch such an endearing and caring woman as Oprah, who has uplifting programs which show everyone how to love and respect mankind. I would love to meet Oprah someday and tell her how much I respect her grace and love to her fellow man.

Since we are on the subject, I have gained some admiration for, and this may be a surprise to some, and that is the owner of the Dallas Cowboys, Jerry Jones. I bring this up, because I am around a lot of NFL people and have expressed my love of the NFL. Over the years I have met many NFL players because of the amount of time I spend in NFL locker rooms. I can truly tell you that there are many NFL players who are really good people. You hear of many football players who get into trouble with the law, but that is such a small fraction of the NFL players. Most players are caring people with good families and work hard at their profession.

I remember a couple of years back, I spent some time in Dallas on my wife's business trip. I was able to drive around Dallas and talk with people and also to spend some time with friends. They were quick to point out to me that there were a lot of people in the Dallas/Fort Worth area who did not care for Jerry Jones.

Maybe it was jealousy of the billionaire or because some fans feel that he unfairly let legendary coach Tom Landry go as the Cowboys' head coach after he led the Cowboys for over twenty-five seasons. Because I've been able to interview Mr. Jones several times in the Cowboys' locker room, after games against the Eagles, I have seen a different side of this man. He is an intense and passionate man who looks at losing as not being an option. I have lived my life watching and learning from people who are good people, and I work to emulate these kinds of people.

He is a positive person who takes advantage of life and only settles for the best. When I have been in the locker room with the Cowboys after games, I have always seen him, win or lose, communicate with his players and always pat them on the back and build them up. This might explain why under his tenure as the Owner and General Manager, he has won three Super Bowl Championships. Positive support and energy, in my opinion, will always build a winner. Jerry Jones has done this and is probably the reason why the Cowboys are one of the most popular sports franchises in the United States.

One of the things I have most respected, is that this guy is so down to earth and so honest. Ask Jerry a question and he will say it as it is and answer you honestly. In our lives, we should all seek out people whom we respect, like a Jerry Jones and an Oprah Winfrey, and learn from them. They have not become so powerful in their professions by chance but it has been their hard work and doing it their way that has made them so great.

If you were to meet me today, you would never believe that I was once shy in my youth, but through junior high school and high school I was about as shy as they come. I grew up in a small town outside of Philadelphia called Berwyn and also spent many years living in Wyckoff, New Jersey, as well. Some people, and even my wife, looked at me as being cocky, but really I was quiet and shy because of all that was going on in my life.

Through all this, though, I still had great friends and a loving family. I played a ton of sports in both towns and was still able to be a good student. If I did not have the family and friends I had, I could have had a drug problem or drinking issues, but never did. I was lucky that I did not use those substances to hide some of my insecurities. I had too much pride and a will to succeed in all I did to let drinking and drugs be a part of my life. To this day I have never touched any kind of drug except the Paxil I take today.

I attribute a lot of my conquering of my OCD to so many people who have loved me in my life. My greatest cheerleader was my own mom, who was always there to take me to my therapy sessions and doctor appointments, when I was hurting and in trouble. The reason I am the father I am today was because she never gave up on me but told me every day that she thought I was great. Today I am the same way with my two kids because I remembered how much that meant to me.

Even though I was suffering she always instilled in me that I was great and someone special. She still does that to this day. I am 38 years old and she still cares about me as much as when I was a little blonde child running around and causing trouble. I can be driving home from an Eagles game in snow and there will be the call from my Mom late at night making sure I got home safely. I do owe my life to her. I guess I can understand the love she has, now that I have my two little blondes running around my own home causing trouble. These children are a part of me and my wife and I will always love them dearly. As I have gotten older I have realized that it is not the car you drive or the money that you make that make a man, it is the love he shares with his family and friends that makes him who he is.

Later in my twenties after graduating from college, I was able to love a father I once disliked because I was not always a priority to him. He was dying of cancer in my early thirties, but we had some fun times together talking and watching sports, and he had a sense of humor that I will always cherish. Plus before he passed away, he was able in his own way to let me know that he did love me, and that was so important to me. He was able to learn more about what made me tick and learned to really respect me, and he talked about that a lot months before his passing.

Also along the way, I have had friends who knew that I was struggling. It would have been easy for them to walk away from me, but they hung in there. I was always a caring friend and the kind of friend you could go to when you needed one. But I had some high school friends and some college friends who cared about me as much as I did for them. When you are growing up you learn that you will only cross a select group of friends who will truly care for you. When you do, do not let them get away from you because they are hard to find.

I also had some girlfriends along the way who taught me what love was all about and cared for me. Dating women can really teach men about love and caring away from their immediate family and I was so blessed to have some great relationships along the way, before I got married. I have a twin brother and a sister, and through our turbulent times we have always loved and cared about each other. Today, I have a beautiful and caring wife Gretchen, who is my friend, lover, and mother of our kids. We met in college, and she has always accepted me as I am. I have grown with a woman who is one of the most hard-working women I have known, and would take the shirt off her back for anyone.

I have good, positive, supportive people in my life. If you don't have such people in your life, people who accept your OCD and support you, go out and find them because they will change your life. You have enough going on in your life when you are depressed, and not having supportive people around will harm even the strongest of people. Like I mentioned before, when I opened up to some of my closest friends and family that I was diagnosed with OCD, all they did was support me and never made me feel any different, which is very important.

Everyone with whom I have shared my life has always supported me through my OCD. Some people are not fortunate enough to have a support system, and I feel for them. If you ever need a listener, I'm available. My email address is dbwhite20@yahoo.com, so email me and you will have someone because I would not have made it without the love of others. If I can be your strong board to lean on we can do it through email. Believe me when I tell you that you will hear from me and that I want to help people who are reaching out for support.

I remember my psychologist, Bruce, saying to me that it was important I let all who loved me know that I had OCD, because keeping that inside was not healthy. I still hold on to that advice today because if I had not told my loved ones about my OCD, I would have to explain my feelings whenever I would have an episode. Now if something comes up they know how to react to it.

When you are going through it, you do not always want to deal with your situation and then have to explain why you are feeling the way you do. Opening up was a hurdle I had to overcome after hiding my affliction for such a long time. Try it and you will not regret it.

Studies done by the Mayo Clinic and by others have shown that, generally speaking, people who are happier in their family lives and in marriage will live longer. This is a good enough reason for me to make sure that I always surround myself with loving and supportive people.

People who are happy with their families and their marriages have lower rates of cancer, suicide, depressive symptoms, and heart failure. According to a study done by Harvard University, married men were 2 to 3 times less likely to commit suicide, have heart attacks, have cirrhosis of the liver, and have other diseases, than single men. Studies also show that people's mental and general well-being benefited greatly when they had loved ones in their lives, which should not be of any surprise to anyone.

Since OCD has to do with low levels of serotonin in the brain, being among strong and supportive family members and friends is vital to healing OCD. When you are happy, this happy chemical will prosper in your brain. If love is not there, find it as fast as you can because your health and mental well-being are at stake.

Stress is the leading cause of most depression, alcoholism, and drug addiction, and this is quite detrimental to a person's physical well-being. Stress also leads to cardiovascular disorders as well as illness and deficiencies of the immune system. Having good people in your life will help you to stay away from these things. Some of these conditions are hereditary, but many of them are brought on because people are lonely and lacking in self-esteem. With no self-worth, depression will eventually come into your life in some way.

Unfortunately, not everyone is so lucky as to come from a loving family or to be in a happy marriage with a soul mate, and evidence of this is that only about 49% of the couples in the United States stay married. That is sad that at one time two people are so in love with one another but so many of us let that slip away in our lives.

So my advice to anyone suffering from OCD or any form of depression is to make sure you find people who will nurture your soul. Without your soul you have nothing. Even medication and therapy can only do so much to help a person heal, but combine treatment with love and you will get back on track to being healthy again. I only wish that for all of you.

Chapter 14

Exercise and Staying Active

"And in the end, it's not the years in your life that count. It's the life in your years."

—Abraham Lincoln

There was a recent article written on Yahoo News by Amy Norton, that talked what researchers have found that show regular exercise, may in certain situations, work as well as medication. There was a study done on 202 people, who had group exercise and the study showed that these individuals did as well as being treated with a antidepressant drug. This is a substantial finding, because exercising is something that someone who is motivated can do to feel less anxious quite easily. Another group was given a placebo pill, according to Norton, and these adults did not fair as well as the individuals that exercised. In the article Dr. James A. Blumenthal, a professor of medical psychology at Duke University Medical Center, in North Carolina, stated that "there is certainly growing evidence that exercise may be a viable alternative to medication." The reason for this will be mentioned later in this chapter.

Recently I've read some troubling numbers from two authors, Michael Carrera, MSC, and Natasha Vani, MSC. They reported that as many as 340 million people worldwide may be suffering from different forms of depression. That is a number you only hope will shrink as the years pass. Education and learning about depression can help us all to know how to deal with the disorders. A lot of this depression can lead to some horrible medical conditions and many of them have been mentioned in some earlier chapters.

These two authors have said that by the year 2020, depression and severe forms of depression like bipolar disorder, could be the second largest cause of death worldwide.

This is one of the reasons I have seen health insurance companies making huge efforts to make this an important part of their benefit coverages in the United States. Health plans across this country are realizing that if they can deal with depression immediately, lives will be saved and claims will be lower in the end. Societal changes have made people more down and out and depression is something healthcare and hospitals will be dealing with for a long time.

Depression has been known to run in families and can be genetic, as I have mentioned throughout this book countless times. There have been extensive studies with men and women on the positive effects of exercise and brain chemicals called norepinephrine, dopamine, and serotonin, which are terms I have used over and over as well. Exercise whether in the form of walking, running, playing basketball or football or any sport can help increase these vital chemicals in our brains.

Through my studies, I have learned that many people who suffer from OCD may have low levels of these neurotransmitters which can lead to why they are depressed. Norepinephrine helps individuals act on their emotions and it controls physical desires like sleep, appetite, attitude, and stress.

Exercise such as running, playing sports, walking, and bulking up in a weight room can cause levels of these neurotransmitters to rise and can be positive ways to help with depression. Over the past two years, I have made a point of working out or playing in basketball and softball leagues to stay active.

I have always played sports so it has been easy for me to work to not only stay in shape, but knowing that it is something good for my mind has made it more of a reason to continually be in the gym.

Studies have shown that the neurotransmitters dopamine and serotonin can be raised when doing things like listening to rock and roll. That is why when I am at the gym I listen to groups like AC/DC, Guns N' Roses, Sammy Hagar, and others to pump myself up mentally and physically. Also sports like basketball, soccer, hockey, and high intensity sports can spur the levels of dopamine and serotonin in the brain.

People sometimes do not look at walking as a good form of exercise. But walking can burn a lot of calories and if religious it can be a great time to talk with God, and in your mind, construct a blueprint of how life is going. Walking is good because it does not put as much wear and tear on one's body like running and some sports do. Walking can give you time to think about work, friends, and family and help a person to "smell the roses" once in a while. Whether you are running or walking, you are getting exercise and you can think about your life.

Carrera and Vani have studied this very subject and have stated that high levels of serotonin and dopamine can effect our emotions and that low levels can cause negative mood swings. Exercising is known to raise the serotonin levels which is why many feel happier and more alert after working out. You will notice that after working out you seem to be able to breathe more freely and your mood seems to be more positive which is good. I know that this is true because in the past it always seemed that when I was in the weight room or playing baseball or football, I could stay more focused and not have my OCD obsessions. I absolutely have enjoyed working out in gyms for many years now and it has been a positive influence that has allowed me to crush many of my OCD symptoms.

It is clearly evident that norepinephrine and serotonin are released during exercise, so we all owe it to ourselves to exercise regularly. Some trainers I have talked with over the past year have said even 30-45 minutes every other day can be very good for people.

A Duke University and Colorado University study, led by researcher James Blumenthal, reported tremendous success with exercise and depression. The study included 156 adults with major depression and the results were impressive. After sixteen weeks of the study, it showed statistically significant improvement in regards to exercise, relative to adults taking the anti-depression medication Zoloft.

After the study, some subjects continued to exercise for as long as six months, and the study showed it was less likely for them to relapse into depression. This is vitally important for people who want to exercise regularly, instead of being put on medication. Before ever considering going off an antidepressant though, make sure you check in with your doctor or therapist. Blumenthal stated that "for each 50 minute increment of exercise, there was an accompanying 50 percent reduction in relapse of depression."

Huge news that came out of the study was that patients who took the medication and who exercised, responded better than the patients who just took medication. Blumenthal said the reason this may be true is that some who want to get better exercise to get better, but "taking just a pill might be very passive."

It has been noted that additional research is still being done to completely link rising levels of these neurotransmitters to exercise, but for now it does seem to have some clout. I know that I have always been heavily into sports and weight lifting, and my OCD barely ever was a factor while I played sports. I do not know if I can contribute this to my mind being focused on something else or if chemically in my brain things were going on. I was drawn to sports particularly in my youth because when I played sports I was free and would not get caught up in any obsessive thoughts. Though after the sport game would end sometimes my anxiety and fears would come back.

It was as if my brain would forget about the obsessions when I was asked to stay completely focused. So I am an extreme believer that working out and exercising in whatever manner you can, is something that can be important for us all. Not only is it more healthy for you, but it seems to show that mentally you benefit from it as well. Sports can build your confidence and self-esteem when you succeed, so I do not know how this cannot be true. So let's all get out there and walk or run and stay active.

I'm 38 now and busy with a family, working for the Eagles, and maintaining a benefits sales position. Still, I have made it a prerequisite to lift and to be on a treadmill a minimum of three days a week—not only to stay in shape but to also stay mentally fit. When I go to the gym, I love to have either a smoothie or a protein shake before working out, and I always have a banana mixed in them because of the serotonin and potassium in that fruit. I always wear a CD player that will play energetic music so that my body can remain pumped up throughout my workout.

A huge fad now is the drinking of energy drinks to help an athlete be given an edge over a competitor. The two drinks I love are Red Bull and Monster Energy, because they taste great and have some good ingredients in them. Even though these drinks are high in fructose, many of them have good levels of B-Vitamins, Ginseng, Gingko Biloba, and other minerals that are great for the mind and body. I love Monster Energy drinks in particular, because I like the low-carb drink with only 10 calories in its content. As mentioned, the drink is packed with Ginseng, which protects against stress and gives additional strength and endurance to its drinkers.

Make sure you check the ingredients though because it does contain glucose and fructose, which could effect people with diabetes. There is also a lot of B6 and B12 vitamins in the drink, which can enhance one's positive mood. Never do I lift weights without my Monster Energy drink for powerful energy and a great frame of mind. Visit them at www.monsterenergy. com.

Try a regular workout regimen if you can, and I guarantee you will feel better than you did the week before, if you were not working out in any manner. All you have to do is read any fitness magazine and you will see countless articles on the many benefits of working out. It is great for your heart and brain and your physical well-being. It can help your body to age a lot more slowly and we all want that for our lives. If you have any medical conditions that limit you from working out, talk with your doctor or trainer at a gym to find both your limitations and what you can do to stay healthy to beat your depression.

Chapter 15

Procrastination and Staying Organized

> *"Procrastination is the art of keeping up with yesterday."*
> *—Don Margeas*

There are so many things in life that can make people's lives so much easier. But, due either to laziness or a lack of organization, many do not choose to take steps to make their lives easier. Over the years, when I had OCD, or even today, I have found that staying organized is vital in helping many OCD sufferers deal with their condition. People with OCD like to have control of their lives and by staying organized you can feel so much more at peace in your life. As a child, I was able to accomplish so much in school and in sports because I was a "list person." A "list person" was the name given to me by my Mom because she knew it was the only way I could get things done daily.

I listed things nightly that I needed to do at school or after school the next day so that I could stay on top of accomplishing all that I wanted to do. My mind and my psyche were always at a high when my list was completed and I felt organized. Most of the time I would not be able to sleep until they were all done. I had little yellow Post-it notes on mirrors in my room. They would allow me to stay on top of the things I wanted to complete each and every day.

For me, it was my way to stay organized, and I would not feel out-of-whack if things were being done. Part of having OCD is that people with the condition like to complete tasks before moving on to the next step in their life. By making lists and checking things off you will not only be more organized but you will feel great in your mind. As I got older and got into the business world I started to use a Franklin Covey Planner, which has helped me become successful in business. The planners have calendar pages in them with plenty of room with the date and times for someone to clearly list all their appointments. I have used the book for probably fifteen years, after a company paid for me to train with the book to stay organized. I have used it ever since. Now that Blackberries are the new wave in communications used by business professionals, I need to get one and use it for scheduled appointments and emails.

Procrastination is often not an option for someone with OCD because he/she will become very anxious if things do not happen in an orderly way and if he does not complete his tasks.

Procrastination is an uncomfortable and frustrating habit that can prevent you from achieving abundance according to Carol Look, author of *Attracting Abundance with Emotional Freedom Techniques*.

"A lot of people procrastinate because they are angry or frustrated with someone. Others don't believe in themselves and feel reluctant to get started," says Look. Trust me when I tell you that if you have a cluttered desk or are a person who is commonly late for appointments or do not return phone calls, look into Franklin Covey books and calendars. I think they are one of the best in what they do.

To this day, I still make lists nightly for the next day's tasks of what I want to accomplish in my personal and professional life. I also put doctors' appointments and personal things in there to help myself feel good and prioritize the things I need to do in my life.

I have found over the years that clients and people have told me that I was psychotic in my follow-up to their needs and wants, so I guess I have found a positive aspect of having OCD.

I have turned a negative into a positive in feeling good that all tasks are completed.

I brought up this point of lists and staying organized for two strong reasons. OCD people, as I call them, are not always made to tackle a lot of things at one time, and being unorganized can lead to constant stress in your life—which is the last thing that someone with OCD needs or desires. With this stress, one can have heightened OCD obsessions and rituals that can drive people crazy.

On a positive note, in my experience the OCD people whom I have known are people who have a lot of drive and conviction. Because of the fighting that they have had to do to cure themselves of OCD, they have learned to be fighters also in their jobs or careers. They know that emotionally they are struggling, and they overcompensate by working harder than most others to succeed in life. You would be surprised to learn of the many great executives today who have overcome OCD and depression to live very productive lives. Many are lawyers, salespeople, doctors, and stock brokers, and they are rock solid people, who are working hard daily to survive with their OCD.

So whether it is a palm pilot, a software calendar, Post-it notes, or day timers that can help you to stay organized, I would make it a part of your life right away. Staying organized is so important for people to take care of themselves and to stay away from their unwanted stress, which is what we are trying to accomplish here. Organize your life and you will see, like I have, that this seems to be something so minimal but it really is something big.

Chapter 16

Support Groups

"If you have an hour, will you not improve that hour, instead of idling it away?"

—*Lord Chesterfield*

I mentioned in an earlier chapter the benefits of seeing a psychologist and/or a therapist to help with OCD and depression. I would recommend seeing a psychologist to anyone because a mental health professional can really help someone who is open to asking for help. They have worked with many clients in the past and been through a lot with a lot of people and can help you. Many of us with OCD have kept our uneasy and anxious feelings inside for such a long time. Having someone to open up to is nice and can really help you fight anxiety and in understanding yourself.

I believe with every ounce of my soul that the therapy I got and the Paxil I took are what made me whole again. I am now able to wake up every day and feel like I have complete control of my life. I am a happy person and feel that I want to conquer whatever life brings my way every day. I now dictate my own life and its direction, and it is not the OCD that controls my life.

As I was writing this book, a very close friend of mine called me because he was having some marital problems. He is separating from his wife because they have lacked intimacy in their marriage for a while. He was also extremely anxious because his job was not going well. It seemed like his life was caving in on him and he came to me for much needed advice about his life. Because of these two things going on in his life, he had become very depressed and reached out to me and asked me for help because of all I had gone through in my own life.

I listened to him and just let him fill me in on everything that was going on in his life. I told him that I really believed that it was time for him to talk with a therapist and also come to terms with his marriage by talking with his wife. Because of writing this book, I was able to direct him about much of my research and some great things he could do to capture his life back.

I told him that sometimes people have their pride and that they will not always reach out for help, but that I thought he needed to do so. I did tell him though that I was so glad that he was comfortable enough to confide in me all that was going on in his life. He did start to see a therapist and also went for a doctor's appointment, and I was glad that I could support him. His doctor did put him on an antidepressant due to the length of time he had been depressed. I learned on that day that sometimes the best support group or person can be your own friends.

The doctor substantiated my advice and put him on Zoloft for depression and anxiety, and also gave him another medication for his depression. When I heard he was put on two different kinds of medications for anxiety, I realized he was really in need of help. As time has passed I have seen such a change in my buddy, who has a great job with a great company in New York City.

My friend said that after two weeks of taking the medications, he really felt that the edge was taken off and that he was feeling better. He was also able to use his medical insurance at his job and started seeing a therapist two times a week. I think for a long time he tried to ignore his anxiety and sadness inside himself, but it finally caught up with him. I encouraged him and told him that as his friend I was proud of him for finally realizing he could not beat this on his own.

If you live in an area where support groups for OCD are nowhere to be found, friends can be a lifesaver. If you have friends who love you and care about your well-being, they are great to get together to talk with and to get advice. People suffering with depression or with OCD, a lot of the time, will reach out for help because they are scared to death with their bizarre thoughts and insecurities with their lives. If you are a good listener always be there for the person or work with them to talk with a professional. It can change their life.

We all, hopefully, have friends who would drop what they are doing to help a friend in need. I have friends who, after I opened up to them, became even closer because I was mature enough to say I was hurting and they have helped me greatly. So if you have one or some of these people in your life, reach out to them and you may be surprised what they can do for you. You may also be surprised to find out that they were themselves depressed at one time or have had their own issues that you never knew about.

If you are a private person or someone who does not want to involve friends in your issues, you do have other outlets. I've discovered a great website called Anxiety Disorders Association of America (www.adaa.org). This is a nonprofit group out of Silver Spring, Maryland, and they have phone numbers you can call if you are looking to talk with counselors about your problems. They can help you find a therapist in your region of the country for you to talk with if you are having a problem finding a counselor to talk with. So realize that you can seek out support groups in your area or online, and that if you reach out to them they are there for you. You will even find in the local section of your newspaper listings for support groups that are right in your own communities for things like depression, drug addiction, alcoholism, etc. You can go to the support groups and talk with others who feel the same way you do and probably spark up some new friendships. Remember that like attracts like.

The most impressive thing that I saw on their website was that they have a database of all the states in the United States. This database lists all the support groups in your area. It clearly lists the different groups, their locations, and phone numbers and what the support group specializes in at their meetings. There are some support groups for OCD and some for panic disorders and some for different kinds of phobias.

These kinds of groups would enable you to talk with people who are just like you, and the groups could change your life forever. The site also has listings for annual conferences that you can attend to talk with professionals and listen to speakers to learn about your condition. There is no reason to be ashamed of your depression at all. Deal with your situation and by talking with others who suffer from your same disorder, you realize that you are no different than a lot of other people.

In addition, the site lists the different disorders and what they are. It can help you to self-diagnose yourself or to help someone else, perhaps a friend or family member, who may be suffering. The site also lists the different modes of treatment such as behavior therapy, medications, and relaxation techniques. Some of the relaxation techniques that they talk about like yoga, meditation, and peace walks, are things I want to start to do more of in my own life. The more you understand OCD, the better you will be able to help yourself.

I remember that when I would go to some of my therapy sessions, my psychologist would have me close my eyes and really relax. He would have me clench my hands and close my eyes and stay completely still from my feet to my head. I would focus on not moving for as long as I could, and I would envision myself lying on a beach and listening to the waves crashing onto the sand. This would help me to relax more than you could ever imagine, and it has been helpful in times of heightened anxiety.

Another great and well-known group is the Obsessive

Compulsive Foundation (www.ocfoundation.org). This group was mentioned in countless books that I read, because of its continued dedication to helping people with OCD and the group's popularity continues to grow. They too have special events and workshops in different states for those seeking help with OCD. This site is great for people with OCD because it predominately focuses just on this disorder. There is a glossary of terms that have to do with OCD, and they too have several search engines that can help you find therapists in your area.

Quite honestly, I found this site to be so helpful in understanding my OCD and finding ways in which I could get help. This foundation clearly defines OCD and ways you can heal. The President of the OCF (Obsessive Compulsive Foundation) seems to genuinely be interested in helping others, because of having a son with OCD. I was able to speak with her and she also told me that she had some OCD issues while growing up and really understands the fears its sufferers have. That is probably why this website is used by so many people worldwide.

Please take some time to check out both of these groups by visiting their excellent websites. Both of these sites will help you with finding the therapists you can talk with and workshops you can attend. Both of these sites have been exceptional resources for me, and I know that they can be for you as well. I am sure there are countless other sites you will be able to find just by surfing the web on your own. Most importantly, take the time to get involved with a support group if you are lucky enough to have one near where you live.

Chapter 17

Sex and Intimacy

"Great sex is great, but bad sex is like a peanut butter and jelly sandwich."

—Billy Idol

"Sex is one of the 9 reasons for reincarnation. The other 8 are unimportant."

—Henry Miller

As I have grown through the years, I have learned so much about relationships and the beauty of a loving relationship. Some of the happiest days of all our lives involve loving relationships. There is the old adage that says, "You can count on your two hands in your lifetime the number of people who truly might love you." I think that might be true and for someone with depression, a loving relationship is quite important. But to get love you have to be able to give it. If you can do that you will be so supported in life and there are times when you will be asked to be there for someone else.

Research done at Cornell University in Ithaca, New York, has showed some substantial evidence that supported the belief that individuals in committed relationships were some of the happiest people. The researchers also found that even those individuals in only casual relationships, reported being happier than those not in romantic relationships.

Continued research is showing that intimate relationships with sound sexual relations, allow people to lead a healthier life. All of us have been in loving relationships in marriage and/or with a girlfriend or boyfriend, and some of them were the happiest days of our lives. When you are intimate with another person and both of you can feel it down to your soul, your emotional state and well-being can really benefit. You feel like you can accomplish anything and life just seems to flow when you are in love. I think love can be an integral part of helping people move past their OCD and depression.

According to an article in 2006 from a magazine called *Body & More*, relationships that are strained can lead to things like back pain (and I am not talking about the pain in the rear brought on by a loved one), minor irritable bowel syndrome, heart disease, and slower recoveries from surgeries. There is something in the makeup of all of us that will benefit from being with a loved one. If you are reading this book and you have been through a recent divorce or breakup just know that there are so many other great people out there looking for the same thing you are. Worry about your own well-being and then a relationship will just move on into your life. It has happened to us in our lives.

The article also talked about the fact that dermatologists will even tell people to get skin cancer screenings more frequently if they do not have a loved one in their lives, because spouses and loved ones notice skin changes more than people do on themselves. I completely believe this study. Basically when you are in a committed relationship, your loved ones will notice any changes on your body and in your mind probably before you will. They will do this because they love you and could not function without you in many cases. That is neat.

My own wife will point out imperfections on my own skin all the time. This is particularly true of the back, because you cannot see changes there. A healthy relationship is, in my opinion, another core to recovering from depression, because if you do not have that, you will be in this battle of life alone.

Duke University conducted another important study, and the results of this study emphasized something that we all need to think about. The study found that 50 percent of single people with heart disease passed away within five years of the evaluation that they had with the doctors at Duke. But, only 18 percent of the people who were in a relationship and surrounded by great friends and a spouse, passed away during that same time period. There is a direct correlation between being happy and having good health internally. I think that this says a lot about the need to find the right person in our lives, and someone who can lift us up and enable us to enjoy life. Every one of us likes to have that cheerleader in life.

I am not a psychologist, but I can say that if you are in an abusive relationship or one that completely lacks love, you should get out as fast as you can because your mental well-being is the most important thing that you have. An uncomfortable marriage or relationship is what leads to a lot of the domestic abuse cases we all hear of and probably why so many people are so depressed in this country.

Another great researcher, Steven E. Hodes, a New York City gastroenterologist, substantiates the importance of being in a stable and enriching marriage or relationship. He states that, "There is a correlation between bad relationships and gastrointestinal symptoms for people with emotional distress, unhappiness, lack of love interest, or conflict within personal relationships."

Once again, keep in mind that these are our bodies and they are a gift of God. We need to uphold our physical and mental states over anything we own or prize. Even if you are not in a serious relationship at this time, surrounding yourself with solid girlfriends/boyfriends or friends, can be really healthy for you. When you are healthy mentally and physically, let's admit it, you want to look good and feel good and you want to exercise more and enjoy life. We all have had the good times and the bad times, and that is a part of life, but having a loved one along for the ride is important.

A recent study at the University of Virginia, in Charlottesville, found what is most important to married women. This is extremely important for us men to remember so that we can continue to be in good relationships. Even more than sexual intercourse, what is most important to women is how affectionate and understanding husbands or boyfriends are, and that they want to spend quality time with their women. Men show a lot of their intimacy through sexual intercourse and that is important to women as well, but loved ones have to want to know what is most important to their spouse.

This finding is supported by one of my favorite writers, Willard Halvey Jr., the author of *His Needs, Her Needs*. This book is one I have suggested to many friends and couples because it helps you understand what is important to a man and what is important to every woman. Halvey comments that, "A typical wife doesn't understand her husband's deep need for sex any more than the typical husband understands his wife's deep need for affection." This book is so powerful and one you should pick up because it lists the five things that a man wants in a relationship and five things that a woman so desires.

Halvey mentions that you cannot just work on four out of the five things but you must do all the things that men and women desire on his list to be happy in your relationships.

Since my recovery from OCD, this is something that both my wife and I have come to terms with, and now we are so much more happy in our lives. I use this book as a kind of bible that I can pick up and read to help my life to be filled with more intimacy with my spouse. Pick this book up and you will not regret it.

I have learned so much about love and women over the last ten years of marriage. My wife has always loved me through my faults and has been there for me when my OCD got difficult. In my life, I also had some girlfriends who taught me what being a man is all about and I thank those people from the bottom of my heart. Relationships, whether with a spouse or significant other, can enrich everyone's soul and we all need them.

We have all been in that relationship that allows us to be so happy that you feel like your heart is going to explode. Is there any better feeling? If you are in a great sexual relationship, is there a better feeling then the feel of the person's soft skin and their shallow breath on your face? Don't take that person for granted because they can be hard to find. Holding a person at night and waking up with that special person is something that is wonderful. A casual walk, shopping, or being at a Broadway show or on vacation with a loved one can bring so much happiness to you. Whether you are a homosexual or a heterosexual, we all need to be loved and be able to give love. There is no better serotonin raiser out there than being in love, in my opinion.

Sometimes, during depression or difficult times, we may have pushed people away, but we have to let loved ones know that we will be back. Sometimes, we just need a break for a while to be by ourselves but loved ones will always be there for us. If you do not have your own soul and mind you will not be able to be there for someone else.

When this happens, assure your loved ones that fun will evolve again and that sexual interest will also come back. When you're depressed, your sexual drive may be compromised anyway, so let your partner know that you still love her or him.

The support and love you will get from loved ones will be crucial to your making a full recovery. Antidepressants can curb your sexual desires a lot and if they do, check in with a doctor because he may be able to change your prescription. And in times of severe depression, you may need some space to find your life, so loved ones need to give you the space that you need.

I cannot express enough the importance of surrounding ourselves with a significant other or with your own children, who will take you for who you are. I can truly tell you that I would not be where I am today without the love of my own family, wife, and my children. They have been the rock that has allowed me to walk away from OCD and to feel so good inside.

I want this so much for you, the readers, because I have been where you are now with the pains of depression, and I want to encourage each and every one of you to be around good people. Hanging around with selfish and uncaring people will lead to your demise. Unfortunately, a lot of people do not realize this until it is too late in their lives. Love yourself because you are truly a miracle.

Chapter 18

Positive and Unending Energy

"The trick is to make sure you don't die waiting for prosperity to come."

—Lee Iacoccio

Early in this book, I mentioned a great moment in my life. That moment occurred when I read a book by Jon Gordon called *The Energy Addict*. I was coming home from a business trip and the title of the book caught my attention. It is a book that has truly changed my life for the better. If you have the makeup and the desire to change your life now, not later, and to become more healthy, you need to add this book to your library.

Jon's newest book is called *The Energy Bus*, and it is such a positive story about a guy who gets a flat tire and has to drive to work on a bus for two weeks. When his car goes into the shop they find out that luckily it did because now they have found some brake issues that could have caused an accident or maybe killed him in the future.

The book talks about the people this man meets and how they are filled with positive energy and they help the man to live a more productive life by thinking positive thoughts. This enables this man to have a better marriage and a better work experience. I am not putting a pitch in for this book because Jon and I have become friends. I mention the book because Gordon can help you to look at life in a different way.

You can walk this earth and carry a positive or negative energy force field around you, and this is the message of the book. The choice is totally up to you. Since I read this book, strong and powerful energy has really led to even more of a positive life for me. My professional life has flourished like never before, my marriage is good, and I have become a better Dad for my own children.

About two years ago, I flew to Jacksonville, Florida, to spend a couple of days with Jon and his family. I was curious, as anyone would be, to see if this hot new author stood by his word and if he was genuine. I took off from the Philadelphia Airport and said to myself that if he was genuine, then I would make a change to my life right away as soon as I got home. It was a soul-searching adventure that I wanted to take in my life, and after meeting him my life since then has seen only good things. I was a positive person before that but Gordon taught me some better things I could do to enrich my life further.

I met my match, in that he had as much of an A-Type personality and was definitely as much of a high energy guy as I. To my surprise, I would later learn that he is a spiritual man as well, because he had prayed to God one day and asked for a better life and God gave it to him. Now Jon feels that he owes it to people to feel the grace that he now feels in his own life.

Jon had lived his life in Atlanta, Georgia, working for a successful computer software company and just plain hated it. He was driving his own wife crazy because he had a negative attitude, and he was later let go by the company. His wife was unhappy and was thinking about moving on with her own life unless he made changes in his life. He knew deep in his soul that he needed a change in his life.

So, he moved to Ponte Vedra, Florida, bought three Moe's Southwest Grille restaurants, and became a National Energy Coach and author. Once in a while you will see him on "The Today Show" with Matt Lauer, directing people on how to live more energized and productive lives. He should be commended because he did not just settle for his life but made a great life for himself and for his family.

He continues to cross the country, doing seminars and talking to many Fortune 500 companies. He has spoken to the Super Bowl Committee, PGA Tour, and the management team of the Jacksonville Jaguars as well as companies such as GE and Cingular Wireless. If this energy person is not a success story then who is? I am glad that to this day I can call him a friend.

Jon has mentioned countless times that if you constantly think positive thoughts, there is no room in the brain for negative thoughts. Since I've been on Paxil, and have changed my thought patterns, there are days I literally feel that I can do anything that I put my mind to.

I guess that is because my medicine is packed with chemicals to raise serotonin and in turn I feel more positive about life. The creativity and the energy will flourish, if I am positive in my life. No person is going to be positive 100% of the time, but imagine if you could do it 90% of the time. You will pass so many people by because as you are happy and succeed at one thing you will look to conquer something else that will make you so much more happy in life.

You could get that job you have always wanted, fall in love, buy a new home or boat, volunteer somewhere, or be a better employee. When you thrive on positive thoughts, you stay away from negativism and make the most out of life. I have done this the last couple of years of my life and it does work.

"We cannot control what happens to us, but we can control what we think about," says Gordon. Jon points this out in his book, *The 10 Minute Energy Solution*, and asks what are your greatest moment of your life? If you can think of these often, you will have only a positive frame of mind. Do not focus on the negative aspects that have occurred in your life because they will only take you to a low place.

Another wonderful author and mentor of mine, who wrote many elequent books on positive energy was the great Norman Vincent Peale. Although I never met the man, I have watched some film on him and he was a humurous man and a man that was so greatly admired by so many. He was a man that believed what determined your happiness was the state of your mind. Peale is someone I started to read and treasure a year ago after reading his critically acclaimed book, The Power of Postive Thinking. The book really touched me and helped change the way I looked at life. He was a minister in a New York Chruch for 50 years and was also a owner of Guideposts magazine, with his wife. Peale lived to be 95 years old and unfortunately passed away in 1993. He was a common man that wrote books for the ages and preached on how you can grow up loving God and thinking positively. If you read his 46 books and I am sure people will for centuries, your outlook on life will forever change for the better.

When I look back on my own precious life, the greatest moments for me are conquering OCD. I knew when I was down before, that I would pick myself up. This is why I am writing this book today, because you too can feel this way. Getting married to my wife, and the births of our beautiful and healthy children also rank way up there as well.

Another huge highlight of my life was the day I walked around the Nova Care Center and the Philadelphia Eagles' office, and was offered a job with them in Media Relations and Public Relations. That memory makes me smile inside and out for a long time. My boss, Bob Lange, has always treated me with respect and helped me to love being with the Eagles. When I work with the Public Relations Department on game day I am as happy as I have ever been because I am doing something that I love. A deep-seated passion of mine is to work for an NFL team on a full-time basis, and I have no doubt I will make that happen some day. What you think about and desire will eventually happen to you.

Seek out your passions in life and what drives you in life and in your job. Get self-absorbed sometimes in hobbies, work, modeling, music, the arts, writing, or whatever. You are the only one who can make the chapters of your life a great story. What are your memories and accomplishments? Think of them often and your life will change. As your depression subsides, reach out to others and do the same for them. Pass it on. When you are positive, people just seem to flock your way.

The world has become so negative. You repeatedly turn on the TV and see people of all colors and creeds killing one and other. It seems like so many countries across the world are fighting religious wars, that you begin to wonder if the world is coming to an end. You wonder why so many people have become withdrawn and depressed, and, if they are really down, sometimes resort to suicide. The world seems to have become a selfish world unlike the way it was when my own parents were growing up. They seemed to have respect for people other than just themselves. Somehow we have to get back to that.

Gordon writes in his book about "Energy Vampires." This has become a term I have used and thought about so much since the day I read it on the pages of his book. Energy vampires are people who are pessimistic and negative in life and are there to try to bring us down. It does not take a brain surgeon for anyone with OCD or who has been diagnosed as being depressed, to realize that you cannot be around people like this.

Gordon says in his book that these vampires can be anyone—teachers, family members, coaches, loved ones. If you run into energy vampires, hold up garlic in their face and run from them as fast as you can. If you love these vampires, ask them for a favor and that is to ask them to change, if they want you around. If you can learn to do this, the energy within you and your soul will only prosper. People, in my opinion, have to surround themselves with the friends, work associates, and family members who will strengthen their will and well-being.

Jon has been an inspirational figure who came into my life after I emailed him one time after reading his book. That is one of the reasons that I too will put my email address out there. I owe it to people to give to them like he did to me one day and it changed my life for the best. His writing and his seminars have changed the man that I am and it can do the same for you. Jon is a friend, sure, but my intentions were not to promote him but to bring a philosophy to you, the reader. If he changed my life he may be able to do the same for you. If you could tie this message to your therapy sessions or with taking your medication for depression, we could all live in a better world years from now.

Chapter 19

Good Stress and Stress that Kills

"I know a lot of men who are healthier at age fifty, than they have ever been before, because a lot of their fear is gone."

−Robert Bly

We have all had many times in our lives when we've experienced stress in some way, and there is truly good stress and bad. I can remember taking the SATs in high school and having a knot in the pit of my stomach because the test could dictate the college I went to and my future. I can remember taking my driver's test, and when the instructor asked me to turn on the headlights, I could not remember where the switch was. There is stress that can drive up our adrenaline and make us soar to new levels in our life.

Plus, many of us who play sports get that butterfly in our stomachs before a big football, baseball or softball game, or in any sport. Stress can be good in that it makes you more attentive to what is going on in your job or in sports, and it can help you be more focused.

You can see this whenever you are watching someone like Tiger Woods play golf. Undoubtedly, he is the greatest golfer who has ever played. He is nervous inside, but you would never know it because he finds focus and energy with his stress and it helps him excel. So there is some good in stress in our lives, but stress can also kill people who do not know how to handle it.

Today, as I was writing this section of the book, a news

report came out that superstar and flamboyant receiver Terrell Owens, wide receiver for the Dallas Cowboys, may have tried to commit suicide by taking many pain killers. It was later reported though that Owens had by accident mixed his pain killers with some health supplements he takes and it caused a reaction. Many of the teams he has played for were concerned about his mental state and some of the teams pushed him to see a team psychologist. There is no doubt that athletes of Owens' status are always under a lot of stress from fans and from the media, who watch every step they take. I can only imagine what Owens would be if he was to focus all his energy to being a good person and focus on the positive things in his life.

The first feelings that came to me were of complete sadness and concern for another human being. Owens has been fighting an internal battle within himself for a long time, and when it came out that they thought he had tried to commit suicide, I thought it had finally caught up with him. I do not know if Owens has depression, but if it comes out ever that he does I hope he takes complete care of himself. He has been blessed with such a great talent and if he could stay away from complaining and the negative things in his life, he could not be stopped on the football field.

He was known by many as a loner, a kind and shy person, and he may have been hiding something, even though it has been reported that many of the teammates who he has played with have liked him. Owens is an extremely dedicated athlete and is extremely competitive and for that I can respect him. This is proof of how powerful the human mind is and that even if you have all the money and popularity in the world, you may not be happy inside. I do not know if he is happy inside or not.

It also shows that everyone needs to have special friends in life and to surround yourself with people who care about you. You need these kinds of people in your life when you are in trouble. I only pray that Owens is humbled and learns to take care of his mental state as much as his chiseled body.

Over the many years of my life, I, like many, have faced many stressful situations of my own. From the time that we all enter this great world we are going to have stress in our lives, and some can deal with it better than others. Let's face the hard reality that stress is a part of our life and it always will be. Whether you are terminally ill or disabled, or have suffered the loss of a loved one, or are going through a divorce or a breakup, stress is a part of us all. And frankly, it will always be a part of our lives.

Surviving stress, though, can in a strange way make us better people. I went through so many years of stress from my OCD, but it made me who I am today and now I want to help others. My first passion is to someday work in the NFL full-time, but my second is to make sure that others can be saved from the ill effects of OCD.

I encountered a lot of stress, as you have seen, in my youth with the divorce of my parents and the loss of my twin brother, who moved to live with my father when we were young. It was painful that he and I were not able to grow up and play more sports together and walk the same halls in high school. But in the end these episodes in my life have made me the man I am today. I am not perfect but I am a person who has found myself. Some people live their whole lives and never find out who they really are.

Also, OCD, the fear of death, and the fear of having different diseases brought a tremendous amount of unwanted stress to my life. Now that I am healthy and without fear of these unwanted thoughts, I continually go the extra mile to give myself a lot of extreme self-care. This is a term I have learned from one of my favorite authors, Cheryl Richardson, who is on Oprah frequently and who wrote *Stand Up For Your Life*. She always talks about making sure you check in with yourself and giving your precious body and mind extreme self-care. We all need this once in a while in order to function.

I feel that I owe my body a lot of self-care because of the stress I brought to it growing up with OCD. I am not a big drinker of alcohol and have never messed with any kind of drugs. Drugs and alcohol can help one to feel better for a couple of hours, but they are just a band-aid on a more serious emotional and mental issue that a person has. I am not perfect though, in that when fishing or playing some sports I do dip Skoal once in a while and I am not proud of that. But like anything else in life anything in moderation is ok.

A recent story from Reuters in London came out and it said that the number of middle-aged men drinking themselves to death has doubled in their country since 1991. The story said that men between the ages of 35 and 54 have suffered the largest rise in deaths with alcohol. The deaths have doubled among middle-aged men to 30 per 10,000 of the population. I am sure this is probably true here in the United States. Stress can probably be most attributed to the alcoholism problems in both countries, and if you do not take care of yourself mentally you will not be able to heal. The report also showed the same thing for women between the same ages.

Drug addiction and alcoholism over the past 40 years are so much more prevalent. A lot of this is attributed to the stress people have in relationships, marriages, at work, and in their lives. Sooner or later this has to change. People need to face their stress head on and deal with what is troubling them or the future looks quite bleak.

I have forced myself to eat better and to work out three to four times a week. I love to take supplements like St. John's Wort, Vitamin E, and Omega-3 to energize me and allow me to feel wonderful. Sometimes it takes a lot to make changes to your life but you have to make those changes to be happy. As you heal from depression, make this a part of your life. Sometimes eating healthy is tough and getting to the gym seems like such a chore.

But if you do it regularly it will just be a way of life. Heightened episodes of stress in your life will kill your immune system and only worsen the effects of OCD and depression. My bouts with OCD were always at their worst when stress was in my life. Stress can trigger heart attacks and irregular heartbeats that can kill. So make changes today and do not wait till tomorrow. Your life is at stake here.

Some common symptoms of stress, besides heart ailments, are aching muscles, headaches and migraines, backaches, nervousness, sweaty palms, and upset stomachs to name but a few. When my OCD was at its worst, I would worry about insignificant things and worry about my health endlessly and this would make me very tired. I am sure we all have felt like this along the way, but if it lasts for days or weeks, get help immediately. Your body is trying to tell you something, and we all have to listen to our inner being.

I think that in my teens and early twenties, I was not mature enough to realize that my body was speaking to me and saying, "Slow down or else." As I have grown up, stress has not been as big in my life, even though I have two kids now and my job is demanding and I have so many more responsibilities in my life. I have learned to prioritize what is really important in my life.

I attribute a lot of this to the serotonin being regulated in my brain and the drastic changes I have brought to my life. These have changed my emotions, my moods, and my brain functionality.

Unfortunately, in my life I have had some friends with drug and alcohol addictions who have ruined their lives. Seeing the destruction it brought to their lives has helped me see what stress can do to someone's life. As mentioned earlier in this book, I have had a couple of people I have known commit suicide because of being bipolar and not properly taking care of themselves as they should. They had stress that could kill and it eventually took their lives. I do not want to have any other people around me fall to that fate.

It seems that today people are moving so fast and trying to outdo the next person that many of them have forgotten to stop and check in with themselves and their mental states, and this is sad. We owe it to ourselves, and believe me I have had to realize it as well, that we need to slow down and take personal time with ourselves to truly understand who we are.

Many of my friends have commented recently that I have always seemed so optimistic and upbeat, and they never knew I had OCD. I was just so good at hiding it from people and that is probably what brought on so much stress in my life. Inside, I was sad and struggling, but I was not going to let anyone know the way I felt. After all, we all have our pride and succumbing to OCD or any kind of depression is just something I refused to let happen to myself. I am happy today because I worked hard to get myself where I need to be.

I have opened up in this book because there are so many people who have OCD and together we need to beat this disease. If I can help thousands to feel great, like I do now, it will give me the satisfaction that I did something important while here on earth. I really and truly want this to be my legacy because I feel so good now and never really envisioned that I might feel this way.

Over the last five years, my life has pretty much been stress-free. I want the next five years of my life to be the same. Sometimes I talk to myself and say, "Congrats to you because you went through a lot but one day said, 'No, not anymore.'"

Once again, I have to say that we are all captains of our own ships and we are the only ones who can change the course of our lives for the better. You have to reach down really deep and think of all the stresses in your life and eradicate them from your life.

If you have a drug or alcohol problem, pick up the phone today and call your doctor and just say, "I am tired and I need help." Go see the doctor, and if you must, get into a detox center and say, "I am going to beat this no matter how long it takes. My sanity is at stake here and no drug is going to control the man or woman I aspire to be."

I used to beg my Dad to get help so that he could see his grandchildren someday, but he chose to go the other way. He would have eight grandchildren to love and play with today and he never met any of them. That is so sad for him and for my children and for my brother and sister's children that they never got to meet a great man that my Dad was. I am at peace with why he was the way he was and I have reached deep in my heart to forgive him for some of the things he did with his life and mine. Forgiveness is so important and it will help to alleviate so much stress in our lives.

If you have been in an unhappy relationship in marriage or with a significant other, fix it or get out. A great book I read was *His Needs, Her Needs*, by Willard F. Halvey Jr. I would recommend this book to anyone in a relationship. This great author talks about his experience of dealing with couples and how men and women are different beings. If you want to be happy in a relationship you have to realize that plain and simply men and women are different beings and by understanding those differences will only make us better people.

If you are in a violent relationship, which has triggered your OCD or depression, take care of yourself and call a family member or the police and say, "Help me." If you have lost a loved one, go to bed at night and pray to them and let them know you love them with all your heart, but that you need to move on with your life. You know this is what they would want for you.

As a part of your recovery from depression, there is no room for talk, but only action. You will not get better if you do not make depression your priority and seek out the professionals and loving family members who can help you.

I reached out and with all their help, today I am the man I always wanted to be. Make the changes now and not a year from now. You need to say that your life is too important and punch this part of your life in the kisser. You owe it to yourself to do so.

Remember that OCD is a disease and should be treated as one. Just as if you have a horrible disease like cancer, you go for chemotherapy and radiation in the hopes of living a normal life. With OCD you must try to live a stress-free life as much as you can.

We all have vacation time at work. I have worked with so many people who take pride in not using vacation time and are proud of it. Learn to take your vacation days for going to the beach, cabin, or skiing and learn to unite with your soul. Without your soul, you are just bones and skin.

So many of us like to keep on moving in life and do not take the time to smell the roses around us. Getting wrapped up in your family or kids is something I have learned to do, and I am benefiting from it as much as my wife and kids are.

I spent so many hours working in the past with my employee benefits companies, for the Eagles, and playing sports that sometimes I forgot about the most important thing, my family. None of us are perfect and God knows I am not, but at least I saw the writing on the wall and learned to make changes. By making my priorities my family and friends it enabled me to surround myself with great people.

Your spouse and your kids, if you have them, are relying on you to nurture their souls and well-being. Throwing a football with my son or taking my son and daughter boating, has enriched my whole being and brought so much satisfaction to my life.

So, as we all learn to recover from our OCD, make it a priority to stop and evaluate where you are in your life. Rid yourself of the energy vampires that surround you and learn to associate only with good people. If you like going to church open up your heart to God and He will be there for you. He has been there for me whenever I needed Him. Learn to find out what stresses are in your life and change these aspects of your life one by one.

Your brain and mind, and organs like your heart and stomach, are relying on you each and every day. You want them to hold up, so you must take as good care of them as you do your home or your car. You only live once on this earth, unless you believe in reincarnation, and then they are going to bury us all six feet under for a very long time. Make the changes today that will allow you to stay alive longer and your life will be so much less stressful.

Chapter 20

Conclusion

"Joe's gonna be smokin' and I ain't even jokin', but I'll be peckin' and pokin' and I'll pour water on that smokin'."
—Muhammed Ali

"I've never known a man worth his salt who in the long run, deep down in his heart, didn't appreciate the grind, the discipline. There is something good in men, that really yearns for discipline."
—Vincent Lombardi

Discipline, what a powerful word, and one that people should store in the back of their minds as they live. Getting renewed and healthy again will take strong discipline. If you played sports or were in music or art, you knew you had to practice to be successful at what you did to be great. To beat OCD or any depression, you are going to have to be extremely disciplined and be extremely determined. You may get tired working to beat your illness but in the end you will respect yourself that you did it.

Do not put it off for another day. Stand up and look into the mirror and say, "Today!!! Today is the day, I am going to get better and change the course of my life. Nobody is going to do it for me but I am going to have to do it for myself."

Help is out there in different forms and the only thing that could hold you back from beating your depression is laziness. I got better from OCD, and if I did it, I know that you can as well. I wrote this book and opened up my past wounds so others could heal. We are all made the same and therefore a lot of the insecurities I had you may have as well. Together we can get through your issues and I hope after reading this book you learned a lot. I wanted to be as clear as possible about what you needed to do and I hope that I accomplished that.

I have been to the dark side of depression and OCD, and I am not going back. I have decided in my own mind that I am going to do whatever I have to do to live with peace in my soul.

You do not need to go back either, if you discipline yourself to make changes now, you can get better. I am not God, and if I were, I would one-by-one heal each and every person with depression. I have cured myself so much that sometimes I almost forget what OCD felt like—well kind of.

How many of you want to feel as I do? I do not know your condition and the severity of your depression, but take it from me that you will get better because I was bad, really bad, at one time and now I can write about it.

My goal when I set out on this project was to write a short book that got to the point of beating OCD. I read so many books on the symptoms of OCD and what to look for with depression. I wanted to write a book that touched on that, but most importantly I wanted a handbook for people to read purely on how to get healed. Keep this book in your library and if you ever forget some of the things I talked about pull it down and read it again. There was a lot of research and study that went into this book because I wanted to make it right and to help the masses.

There are psychologists and wonderful doctors out there who have been trained to deal with depression and they are good at what they do. Always consult with a doctor if you want to make serious changes to rid yourself of OCD, because they have been through depression with others before. I hope when you put this book down you will have a smile on your face and feel inspired to think about the steps I listed in this book and make changes to your life. Do it now!

Love to all and God Bless You!!!!!!!!!!!!

David White, Lititz, PA
Email Address: dbwhite20@yahoo.com
Book Website coming soon!!!

Please contact me soon if you want to talk and you will be surprised that you will hear from me on email. I stay on top of getting back to people who need advice on the things listed within the contents of this book.

Best Wishes,
Dave

References

1. Gordon, Jon, *The Energy Bus*, 2007, John Wiley & Sons, Inc.
2. Gordon, Jon, *The 10-Minute Energy Addict*, 2006, G.P. Putnam's Sons
3. Bryne, Rhonda, *The Secret*, 2006, Simon & Schuster CD Book, www.thesecret.tv
4. Summers, Marc, *Everything in Its Place*, 1999, Penguin Putnam, Inc.
5. Levenkron, Steven, *Obsessive Compulsive Disorder*, 1991, Warner Books, Inc.
6. Harley, Willard F., Jr., *His Needs, Her Needs*, 2001, Fleming H. Revell
7. Richardson, Cheryl, *Take Time for Your Life*, 1999, Broadway Books
8. Web Md, reference www.webmd.com
9. Gray, John, reference www.marsvenus.com
10. Filer, Wanda, WGAL Health on Your Side newscast
11. (NIOSH) *The National Institute of Occupational Safety and Health*, reference www.cdc.gov/niosh/homepage.html
12. Citrin, Jim, reference yahoo finance, www.yahoo.com
13. Hupe', Pallas, reference www.yahoohealth.com
14. Clevidence, Beverly, reference www.usda.gov
15. Holub, BJ, Omega-3, www.yahoohealth.com
16. Schimelpfening, Nancy, www.depression.about.com
17. OC Foundation, www.ocfoundation.com